AR41

The Lives of Images

PICTURING HISTORY

Series Editors
Peter Burke, Sander L. Gilman, Ludmilla Jordanova,
Roy Porter, †Bob Scribner (1995–8)

In the same series

Health and Illness
Images of Difference
SANDER L. GILMAN

Men in Black
JOHN HARVEY

Dismembering the Male
Men's Bodies, Britain and the Great War
JOANNA BOURKE

Eyes of Love
*The Gaze in English and French Painting
and Novels 1840–1900*
STEPHEN KERN

The Destruction of Art
*Iconoclasm and Vandalism since the French
Revolution*
DARIO GAMBONI

The Feminine Ideal
MARIANNE THESANDER

Maps and Politics
JEREMY BLACK

Trading Territories
Mapping the Early Modern World
JERRY BROTTON

Picturing Empire
*Photography and the Visualization of the
British Empire*
JAMES RYAN

Pictures and Visuality in Early
Modern China
CRAIG CLUNAS

Mirror in Parchment
*The Luttrell Psalter and the Making of
Medieval England*
MICHAEL CAMILLE

Landscape and Englishness
DAVID MATLESS

The Thief, the Cross and the Wheel
*Pain and the Spectacle of Punishment in
Medieval and Renaissance Europe*
MITCHELL B. MERBACK

'Down with the Crown'
*British Anti-monarchism and Debates about
Royalty since 1790*
ANTONY TAYLOR

The Jewish Self-Image
*American and British Perspectives
1881–1939*
MICHAEL BERKOWITZ

Global Interests
Renaissance Art between East and West
LISA JARDINE AND JERRY BROTTON

Picturing Tropical Nature
NANCY LEYS STEPAN

Representing the Republic
Mapping the United States 1600–1900
JOHN RENNIE SHORT

Bodies Politic
*Disease, Death and Doctors in Britain,
1650–1900*
ROY PORTER

Eyewitnessing
The Uses of Images as Historical Evidence
PETER BURKE

The Art of Suicide
RON M. BROWN

The Lives of Images

Peter Mason

REAKTION BOOKS

para Anne Chapman, la que tiene el corazón más grande

Published by Reaktion Books Ltd
79 Farringdon Road, London EC1M 3JU, UK

www.reaktionbooks.co.uk

First published 2001

Series design by Humphrey Stone
Printed and bound in Great Britain by
Bookcraft, Midsomer Norton

British Library Cataloguing in Publication Data

Mason, Peter, 1952 –
     The lives of images. – (Picturing history)
     1. Art, European 2. Human beings in art
     I. Title
     704. 4

ISBN 1 86189 114 8

Contents

Acknowledgements 7

Introduction 9

1 The Lives (and Deaths) of Fuegians and Their Images 19

2 Being There 55

3 From America to Oxfordshire? 80

4 The Purloined Codex 101

5 Images and Objects 131

References 149

Photographic Acknowledgements 171

Index 172

Acknowledgements

The research behind this book was conducted in Santiago de Chile, London, Brussels, Paris, Krakow and Amsterdam. I am grateful to Roberto Edwards and the Fundación América for hosting my stays in Santiago, to Francisco Bethencourt and the Gulbenkian Foundation for doing the same in Paris, and to the members of the various archives and libraries who patiently responded to my inquiries and supplied the original photographs, in particular David Newman of the library of the South American Mission Society at Allen Gardiner Cottage, Tunbridge Wells.

The main argument of the book, as summarized in Chapter 1, was presented as a *ciclo de conferencias* at the Institute of Aesthetics, Pontificia Universidad Católica de Chile, in March 2001 at the kind invitation of Margarita Alvarado Pérez. Its final form has benefited from those lively discussions in Santiago. An early version of Chapter 2 appeared in English as 'En tránsito: Los fueguinos, sus imágenes en Europa, y los pocos que regresaron', in P. Mason and C. Odone, eds, *Culturas de Patagonia: 12 Miradas: Ensayos sobre los pueblos patagónicos*. An earlier version of Chapter 3 appeared as 'Ethnographic Portraiture in the Eighteenth Century: George Psalmanaazaar's Drawings of Formosans', in *Eighteenth-Century Life*, XXIII (1999) – though I would now prefer to write '"Ethnographic" Portraiture'. An earlier version of Chapter 4, written after Arthur MacGregor had tipped me off about the Harman monument and Brenda Kirsch had taken me to Burford, was presented at the conference entitled 'Natura e Cultura: L'interpretazione del mondo fisico nei testi e nelle immagini' at the Accademia Nazionale Virgiliana di Scienze, Lettere ed Arte, Mantua, in October 1996 at the kind invitation of Giuseppe Olmi. It was subsequently published as 'Of Turkeys and Men: Towards a Historical Iconography of New World Ethnographic and Natural Historical Representation' in the volume with the same title as the conference, edited by L. Tongiorgi Tomasi, G. Olmi and A. Zanca (Florence, 2000). A shorter version of Chapter 5 was presented to the Tagung der deutschsprachigen Ethnologinnen und Ethnologen in Vienna in September 1995 at the kind invitation of Adam Jones. It was subsequently published in *Journal of the History of Collections*, IX (1997). The section of Chapter 6 on Humboldt is based on 'Moving Mountains and Raising the Dead', in M. Jansen and L. Reyes, eds, García *Códices, Caciques y Comunidades* (Leiden, 1997).

Although I live and work in Amsterdam, this book was written without support from any Dutch institution. As an independent writer, I am all the more dependent on friends and colleagues for passing on articles and other materials and for making valuable suggestions. It is thus a pleasure to acknowledge the assistance of all those who have helped in various ways: Margarita Alvarado Pérez, Christian Báez Allende, Clare Baines, Nicolas Barker, Christine Barthe, Ernst van den Boogaart, Giancarlo Carabelli, Anne Chapman, Eugenio Dittborn, Jacqueline Dubois, Elizabeth Edwards, Christian Feest, Jean Fisher, Caterina di Girolamo, Paula Honorato, Maarten Jansen, Adam Jones, Geneviève Lacambre, Sebastián López, Colin McEwan, Arthur MacGregor, Pedro Mege Rosso, Carolina Odone, Giuseppe Olmi, Marisol Palma, José Pardo Tomás, Elaine Reichek, Luis Ángel Sánchez Gómez, Ben Schmidt, Claudia Swan, Christel Verhas and Thea Vignau-Wilberg. Muchas gracias.

It has been a pleasure to work with the editorial team at Reaktion, especially Andrea Belloli and Harry Gilonis.

Florike Egmond's contribution is unique. Without it, I would be nowhere. My debt of gratitude to her is boundless.

Introduction

Among the gifts presented by King Manuel I of Portugal to Pope Leo X in 1514, and later depicted by Giovanni da Udine on the stucco panels of the Vatican Loggias, were a cheetah, two leopards, a number of parrots, various Indian fowl, rare Indian dogs and a Persian horse – as well as a four-year-old Indian elephant. Purchased from the King of Cochin by Afonso de Albuquerque, the elephant had been transported by sea from Cochin to Lisbon in the summer of 1511, its hide smeared with oil to protect it from the salt air. Manuel kept it in the royal park of Ribeira before it embarked on its journey to the pontiff, first by land to the harbour of Lisbon, where it reluctantly went on board, then by sea to Porto Ercole in Italy, stopping at various Balearic harbours along the way, and, finally, by land again along the 113 km of the former Via Flaminia to Rome. The crowds and confusion that accompanied the elephant's ponderous journey by land created much destruction en route to the Holy City. On 19 March 1514, the elephant featured in the entry of the procession of obedience, an ostentatious practice of European sovereigns that involved sending an extraordinary ambassador to Rome upon the election of a new Pope. Pope Leo was delighted as the creature gleefully sprayed water from its trunk and drenched him. Annone, as the Romans called him, was kept temporarily in the Belvedere courtyard until a special building could be erected just off the Piazza di S. Pietro. During his stay in the city, Annone performed for the public, kneeling in response to the commands of his mahout, dancing to music and spraying onlookers with water from Rome's many fountains, as well as appearing in the great and notorious carnival held to crown the buffoon Baraballo. The elephant was celebrated in verse, and inns and streets were named after him. On his death (either from an illness or from the purgative administered to cure it) on 8 June 1516, a satirical text purporting to be Annone's last will and testament circulated widely, and the Pope called on Raphael to execute a life-size mural of the beast (which no longer survives) on the wall adjacent to one of the entrances to the

Vatican. Annone lingered metonymically in the Vatican for centuries – his tusks were hung there.

The travels of the elephant himself – from Cochin to Portugal, from Portugal to Rome – are mirrored, if not surpassed, by the travels of posthumous representations of him. While the white marble elephant fountain at the Villa Madama, whose trunk functioned as a water spout, remained on Italian soil, the Haarlem artist Maarten van Heemskerck, who spent three years in Rome in the 1530s, took back to the Netherlands at least two sketches of Annone's head based on this fountain. The visit by the young Portuguese architect and scholar Francisco de Holanda to Rome in 1538–9 prompted him to propose a fountain in the shape of an elephant to the Portuguese monarch, and Francisco's ink drawing, copied from the lost fresco by Raphael, not only transported Annone's image to the Iberian peninsula, but seems to have spread visual information about the Indian elephant as far afield as Africa. Local artists of Sierra Leone, Benin and the Congo, it has been argued, were commissioned to carve works of art in ivory for the Portuguese, who had established commercial bases in the region in the late fifteenth and early sixteenth centuries; these works were executed in accordance with European designs or models to cater for the tastes of European princely collectors. Annone's image has been identified as the visual source for an elephant carved on an ivory horn (or oliphant) in Africa and now in the Musée de l'Homme, Paris. This oliphant is a striking instance of just how far flung the routes taken by images and their subjects can be: in real life or in representation, Annone belongs to the history of India, Africa and Northern and Southern Europe.[1]

As is well known, European artists – famously Dürer – were perplexed by the problem of how to depict non-European fauna. And when those fauna were as volatile as Annone the elephant, something of the rhythm of the exotic subject's movements rubbed off on images of it. Of course, movement was virtually always a part of the exotic representation, whether in the case of an artist such as the Dutch painter Albert Eckhout, whose portraits of non-Europeans in Dutch Brazil in the seventeenth century were based on his travel to and presence in foreign territory, or in the case of the (voluntary or involuntary) movement of non-Europeans to Europe.[2] The situation was even more complicated when images of non-European people or animals in transit were themselves on the move. Chapter 1 deals with such a case: natives of Tierra del Fuego who were taken to Europe and travelled widely (under compulsion) there, and the travels of the images that were made of them.

The earliest European representation of a native of Tierra del Fuego, in an engraving of the scene of Magellan's discovery of the straits that bear his name (the engraving is reproduced and discussed in Chapter 1), also includes a travelling Indian elephant being carried through the air in the talons of a huge bird, the mythological roc, like the great birds or *Rukh*s, also mentioned by Marco Polo, that carried Sinbad into the mountains by his turban and dropped stones on his ship.[3] In his brief discussion of the engraving (published in 1937–8), the art historian Rudolf Wittkower connects this image with representations of the struggle between the eagle and the snake (in Sanskrit epics, the word *naga* means both 'snake' and 'elephant'), to which he devoted a much longer essay in the following year. Wittkower described such images as 'symbols' and 'archetypal images' that we encounter through long periods of time and across wide spaces.[4] Drawing his inspiration from diffusionist ethnology, he combined the tracing of the migrations of such symbols on the basis of European documentary evidence with the postulating of such migrations in cases where the same symbol appeared in a non-European setting, 'even if the connecting links are still missing'.[5] This combination of two different methodologies led to a distinction between two different bodies of material: on the one hand, the relatively well-documented world of European culture since classical times, where it is often possible to determine with a reasonable degree of exactitude the particular meaning (its 'function', to use Wittkower's terminology) that the same pictorial symbol had in each particular historical setting, on the one hand; and, on the other hand, the more scattered and fragmentary material relating to the postulated migrations of the same symbol to India, Polynesia, Scythia, Eastern Siberia and the Americas (where the eagle tearing a serpent sitting on a nopal cactus was the glyph for Tenochtitlán, the centre of Aztec civilization).[6]

Wittkower's work in patiently reconstructing pictorial traditions – especially his classic investigation of the pictorial traditions of the monstrous human races of the East[7] – is invaluable, and the present study is heavily indebted to it. Nevertheless, the migration of symbols is not the same as the lives of images. The swastika, the winged globe, the Tree of Life, the eagle and snake, the Great Mother, the mythical hero as animal-tamer, the dragon and so on[8] are much wider in scope and more diffuse in definition than the images discussed in this book. And the term *images* is preferred here, not only to avoid the Jungian connotations of the 'archetypal image' which were very much in vogue at the time Wittkower was writing[9] but also to avoid the making of *a priori* claims regarding their 'symbolic' or other kind of status.

Similarly, 'lives' is preferred to 'migrations' to avoid that shadowy area of Wittkower's research where no definitely traceable roads of migration can be proven to have existed. For it is not only in the non-European material that links may be tenuous and fragmentary; the European material too is not without lacunae. To illustrate, Wittkower claimed that Stradanus (Jan van der Straet), the designer of the engraving of Magellan mentioned earlier (see illus. 18), 'based his picture of the roc and elephant on an original Persian manuscript in Florence'.[10] Since van der Straet (*c.* 1523–1605), a painter from Bruges, worked for most of his life in Florence, the possibility of his having seen such a Persian representation cannot be ruled out. However, the presence of a similar depiction of a roc and an elephant in a woodcut for Ulisse Aldrovandi's *Ornithologia* (1599) suggests not that that Bolognese naturalist took it from the work of van der Straet, but that they both took it from a common source. The likelihood of their independently having consulted a Persian original is much smaller than that of their having drawn on the work of a Florentine artist such as Jacopo Ligozzi, who is known to have supplied Aldrovandi with natural-historical representations.[11] Whatever may actually have happened, it goes beyond the evidence to speak of the 'migration' of an image from Persia to Italy in this case.

Wittkower's notion of migration implies the metaphor of a flow or current, originating in a source, that bears images or symbols along with it in its directional course, although he was well aware that 'cultural products do not, of course, migrate. People move about and may transport objects across wide spaces.'[12] However, this is not very apt when it comes to discussing the erratic movements of the images (and sometimes of their subjects) dealt with in the chapters that follow. Rather, they are caught up in a movement of ebb and flood, of flux and reflux, now surfacing, now disappearing below the surface again before reappearing somewhere else in the same watery mass. It is an area of knowledge where non-knowledge is commoner than its opposite.[13] For instance, in a fascinating discussion of a number of versions of a sculptural group depicting a winged male figure clasping a female nude, Wittkower notes how almost identical versions of the group could be given titles as diverse as 'the abduction of Cybele by Saturn', 'Le Temps qui découvre la Vérité, or 'Missed Opportunity' while being modelled on Bernini's *Rape of Proserpina*.[14] Consistent with his notion of a point of origin is the application of the term *misinterpretation* to later stages in a chronological chain, but it is not immediately apparent why one and the same figure cannot be interpreted not only as Cybele but also, allegorically, as both Truth and

Chance. As we shall see in Chapter 4, an image of the Aztec ruler Motecuhzoma which was interpreted at a later date as referring to a giant is actually in line with European preconceptions about the gigantic stature of the inhabitants of the New World which antedate that image. As has been argued elsewhere in connection with the method of another art historian from this circle, Erwin Panofsky, the dynamic character of a work of art – the vitality of the image – makes of it a signifying complex that resists articulation in an unambiguous and definitive way.[15] Hence the fixity implied in terms like *misinterpretation* will not get us very far when we are confronted with the heterogeneous forms that certain images can assume in the course of their lives, especially when those lives criss-cross other continents besides Europe.

One cannot refer to Wittkower and Panofsky without mentioning the work of Aby Warburg. All three scholars were influenced to varying degrees by the emerging discipline of anthropology,[16] and there are parallels between Wittkower's enterprise and the union of classical philology and art history with oriental studies advocated by Warburg as a means of understanding 'the inner psychological cohesion of the cultural impulses that emanated from the rim of the Mediterranean basin'.[17] Migrating images form the subject matter of many of Warburg's essays. For instance, the above quotation is taken from the 1926 essay 'Astrology under Oriental Influence', in which Warburg tries to establish the defining role of oriental astrology in the selective assimilation of the heritage of antiquity by means of a (still incompletely defined) migration route: Cyzicus – Alexandria – Oxene – Baghdad – Toledo – Rome – Ferrara – Padua – Augsburg – Erfurt – Wittenberg – Goslar – Lüneburg – Hamburg.[18] Or, in tracing the routes along which ancient superlatives of gesture travelled (the subject of his 1892 doctoral thesis), Warburg established a long migration from Athens by way of Rome, Mantua and Florence to Nürnberg 'and into the mind of Albrecht Dürer'.[19]

There is an inherent tension in Warburg's thinking about the lives of images, which is clearly at work in the (in more ways than one) remarkable lecture on serpent ritual[20] which Wittkower also cites with approval.[21] On the one hand, in considering the interpretation of Pueblo Indian decorative elements and dance, particularly the role of the serpent, Warburg was led to ask himself the question 'To what extent does this pagan world view, as it persists among the Indians, give us a yardstick for the development from primitive paganism, through the paganism of classical antiquity, to modern man?'[22] After reviewing the uses of the serpent in the Bible, in antiquity and in medieval theology, Warburg concluded that

> ... the serpent is an international symbolic answer to the question Whence come elementary destruction, death, and suffering into the world? ... We might say that where helpless human suffering searches for redemption, the serpent as an image and explanation of causality cannot be far away.[23]

Despite the use of particular examples, Warburg's argument is a generalizing, indeed a universalizing, one. This is especially apparent in his attempt to match a threefold progression from primitive paganism, classical antiquity and modern humanity with an evolution from a tactile stage via a symbolic stage to the abstraction of modern conceptual thought.[24] This parallelism is articulated with the conflation of the remote in place (the Hopi) with the remote in time (primeval humanity), though the latter conflation is not peculiar to Warburg; indeed, it had become something of a commonplace ever since the 1871 publication of E. B. Tylor's *Primitive Culture* with its doctrine of 'contemporary ancestors'.

This part of Warburg's thesis can be rejected on two different grounds. First, at a theoretical level, the notion that one can 'read off' the beliefs and practices of our prehistoric ancestors from interpretation of the beliefs and practices of our 'underdeveloped' contemporaries is as ethnocentric as it is chronocentric. In both cases, the constructions we make may tell us a lot about ourselves, but they tell us nothing about either our ancestors or our contemporaries, nor do they reveal any point of similarity between those two categories outside our own projections.[25] Second, Warburg selected a singularly bad example on which to base his argument. At the time of his visit to New Mexico and Arizona (late 1895–May 1896), the Hopi Snake and Antelope ceremony, popularly known as the Snake Dance, was 'far and away the most widely depicted Southwest Native American ritual'.[26] August issues of national newspapers and magazines reported every year on these 'Hideous Rites' or 'Weird Arizona Snake Dance'.[27] It was easier to pin the label of primitiveness on the Hopi because cultures like the Navajo and Apache had been more violently disrupted by European contact, leaving the Hopi's agricultural and artisanal way of life to function as a counterpart to the age-old civilizations of the ancient Near East. Moreover, focusing on the search for the most 'primitive' variant of the dance glossed over the fissures that had emerged in the Hopi communities at the time in response to the US policy of assimilation and land allotment.[28] As in many of Edward Curtis's photographs of North American Indians, historical change was thus kept at bay.[29] And by the 1920s, when Warburg gave his slide lecture, the flood of tourists to the area had driven the Hopi to prohibit the sketching and photographing of the ceremony;[30] John Sloan's satirical etching *Indian Detour* (1927) shows a small group of Native American dancers surrounded by a traffic jam of tourist buses.[31]

To be fair, Warburg himself did not consider this lecture publishable, so we should perhaps not be so hard on him. Moreover, it is thanks to its publication that we can detect a second approach to the lives of images that is, if not incompatible with the first, at least devoid of its universalizing and primitivizing aspects. The passage is here quoted in full:

> About twenty years ago in the north of Germany, on the Elbe, I found a strange example of the elementary indestructability [sic] of the memory of the serpent cult, despite all efforts of religious enlightenment; an example that shows the path on which the pagan serpent wanders, linking us to the past. On an excursion to the Vierlande [near Hamburg], in a Protestant church in Lüdingworth, I discovered, adorning the so-called rood screen, Bible illustrations that clearly originated in an Italian illustrated Bible and that had found their way here through the hands of a strolling painter. And here I suddenly spotted Laocoon with his two sons in the terrible grasp of the serpent.[32]

Here, the art historian is on firmer ground: an image showing how christological thought makes use of pagan serpent imagery is traced back to Italy and resurfaces in a North German church.[33] In a similar vein, Warburg's 'On Planetary Deities in a Low German Almanac of 1519' concludes that what looks like a merely naïve piece of popular literature is in fact 'an artistic production of great evolutionary significance, with a cultural importance that far transcends any mere local interest. It enables us to trace the route travelled by certain images ...'[34]

The art historian Georges Didi-Huberman recalls an experience similar to Warburg's shock of recognition in the Lüdingworth church. While engaging in Warburgian meditations on a Christmas market in the Piazza Navona in Rome, he was struck by the resemblance between a polychrome terracotta figurine from the *mercato dei figurine* and the visceral ex-votos crafted by the ancient Etruscans. The time-scale was staggering: the Etruscan figures were 22 centuries older than Warburg's trip to Arizona and New Mexico, 23 centuries older than Didi-Huberman's trip to the *mercato*.[35] Having survived their owners, these images had occupied a number of heterogeneous contexts. Changes of meaning had crept in over the years, however – the Roman figurine obviously did not have the same function as an ex-voto.

15

This ability of an image to move freely from one context to another has a number of consequences. First, it makes it impossible for us to view the image as an ideological product. Of course, when it enters a specific cultural or historical context, an image can be given an ideological role to play,[36] but when it moves on, it is capable of shaking off this ideological accretion and of fulfilling other, sometimes contradictory, roles. Images can make history, but they have no consciousness of doing so.

Second, their mobility makes it impossible for us to impose value judgements on the aesthetic quality or importance of different images for present purposes, for in the course of time they may occupy contexts of varying importance. Though many, if not most, of the images included in this book would be qualified by some as having no great artistic value, this by no means makes them marginal. The present analyses are conducted in the spirit of Warburg's iconological analysis 'that can range freely with no fear of border guards, and can treat the ancient, medieval, and modern worlds as a coherent historical unity – an analysis that can scrutinize the purest and the most utilitarian of arts as equivalent documents of expression'.[37] As we shall see in Chapter 1, a people like the Yahgan of Tierra del Fuego, who occupied an extremely marginal geographical territory at the uttermost part of the earth, played a by no means marginal role in nineteenth-century thought – as is evidenced by their crucial position within Darwin's scheme of things – and public life – as is evidenced by their presentation at key public events in the capitals of Europe. Incorporated within the Darwinian and popular scientific and cultural discourses, the images of these Fuegians played an equally important role. The eighteenth-century portraits of Formosans discussed in Chapter 2 may not have appeared in a major work of travel literature or ethnography, but this case raises important questions of authority and authenticity. The relatively obscure monument in an English country church described and discussed in Chapter 3 has been taken by some scholars to be the earliest three-dimensional European representation of native Americans – reason enough to devote a chapter to it here. And while the images from Mexican screen-folds or figures in the round discussed in Chapters 4 and 5 may be known only to a limited circle of scholars, the account of their travels includes a number of more familiar names, from André Thevet and Richard Hakluyt to Alexander von Humboldt and Diego Rivera.

Third, the emphasis on the vitality of images and on the need for a style or tone of analysis that is receptive to that vitality rules out the possibility of constructing clearly delineated corpora on iconographic grounds. For instance, the attempt to establish a corpus of visual representations of America, as will become clear in Chapter 3, runs up against the difficulty posed by images that can be said to both belong and not belong to such a corpus. For while it makes sense to speak about the corpus of, say, the oeuvre of a single artist, this kind of positivism is misplaced when it comes to dealing with representations that do not always display stability.[38]

Many of the images discussed here are of non-Europeans. The photographs reproduced in Chapter 1, for example, are mainly photographs of the native peoples of Tierra del Fuego. I have resisted the tendency to label them as 'ethnographic'. This is because when we say that a photograph is either black and white or colour, we are talking about an intrinsic quality of the material support in front of our eyes. The epithet *ethnographic*, however, functions in the same way as an adjective like 'good' or 'bad' – there are 'good' photographs, 'bad' photographs, 'ethnographic' photographs and so on. The quality of being 'good', 'bad' or 'ethnographic' lies in the brain of the beholder; it is not an intrinsic quality of the photograph.[39] And just as what may seem 'good' to one viewer may seem 'bad' to another, a photograph that may be an 'ethnographic' photograph to one viewer may be, say, a portrait of her grandmother to another. This is well brought out in the work *Imaginary Homecoming* by the Finnish photographer Jorma Puranen, who went to Paris to see the photographs of Sami people taken by Prince Roland Bonaparte in 1844, re-photographed them, enlarged them on Plexiglas panels and then reinserted them into the landscape from which they came. For some, this homecoming was quite literal, as many of the photographs were of relatives of Sami families known personally to Puranen.[40] Without wishing to under-play the differences between the photograph and other forms of representation, in this respect the inappropriateness of the epithet *ethnographic* when applied to photographs applies *a fortiori* to other images too.

A word has to be said about the reproduction of photographs of Fuegians and other people on show in the pages of this book. The Greenlanders whose names would now be written Poq and Qiperoq, a painting of whom is reproduced on the cover, are said in the entry to the inventory of the Royal Danish Kunstkammer to have left Green-land for Denmark 'of their own free will', though we may legitimately wonder how much pressure was put on them by Hans Egede of the Colony of Good Hope when he selected them as commercial and missionary agents of the Danish enterprise. Other Greenlanders, however, and the Fuegians discussed in the following chapter, did not go of their own volition: they were kidnapped and taken, sometimes in chains, to be put on show in Europe. I hope the reader will understand that it is not my intention to replicate that act of humiliating display; on the other hand, the very argument of the present book is that images have lives of their own, independent of the intentions of those who produce them or through whose hands they pass. At all events, in the present case I have deliberately excluded any photographs of dead bodies or body parts, and in other respects have kept the presentation of images of people on show down to a minimum. On other occasions I have eschewed their use altogether.[41]

Finally, the tendency of the images under discussion to be constantly on the move also means that their lives may become intertwined, for a time at least, with those of other objects. Although this book is not about the history of collections, in many cases the lives of the images discussed impinge on the lives of collections. Sometimes, the images themselves spent time in a collection, either as works of art or as curiosities. An image may represent an object that was present in a collection for a period of time. It may even be a part of a 'paper museum' like that of Cassiano dal Pozzo. Like images, objects circulated at different speeds and over varying distances both within and between collections, sometimes coming to a sticky end in the melting-pot to make coins or weapons,[42] or exiting a collection when the owner died, as in the case of the Milanese collector Lodovico Settala.[43] Stately collections were not all static all the time.

To sum up, the treatment of images in the following pages does not regard them as illustrations, secondary in importance, mere adjuncts to something else (an artist's biography, a text, a political ideology etc.). They emerge at a certain point and time, they travel, they enter and leave different contexts, they come into contact with other images and with other objects. Now it is time for us to get moving and let the images speak for themselves.

I The Lives (and Deaths) of Fuegians and Their Images

In his laudanum-driven *The Black Robe*, the Victorian novelist Wilkie Collins puts the following words into the mouth of Mrs Eyrecourt as she plans a grand party in her Highgate villa to celebrate the return of her daughter with her bridegroom:

> Tea and coffee, my dear Romayne, in your study; Coote's quadrille band; the supper from Gunter's; the grounds illuminated with coloured lamps; Tyrolese singers among the trees, relieved by military music – , and, if there are any African or other savages now in London, there is room enough in these charming grounds for encampments, dances, squaws, scalps, and all the rest of it, to end in a blaze of fireworks.[1]

This reference to the deployment of non-Europeans in Europe for the purposes of entertainment was highly topical for a novel first published in 1881. The zoo in St James's Park, London, had already hosted the display of two native Virginians along with domestic and foreign animals in the reign of Elizabeth I, and the three Mohawks and one Mahican who visited England in 1710 attracted considerable attention in the metropolis.[2] It was above all in the second half of the nineteenth century that the presentation of non-Europeans got under way on a large scale in the capitals of Europe. At this time, there were only two cities that could boast more than one zoo – Paris and Hamburg – and it was these cities that seem to have taken the initiative in combining animal and human displays within the zoo setting. In Paris, Isidore-Geoffroy Saint-Hilaire's plan to set up a secluded environment where animals could reproduce and be studied under competent supervision was put into practice when the Jardin d'Acclimatation was opened in 1860. (It can still be seen today in a corner of the Bois de Boulogne [illus. 1].) Isidore's son Albert, who was promoted from Assistant Director to Director in 1865, witnessed the virtual collapse of this institution during the Franco-Prussian War and the 1870–71 Commune, but in August 1877 – perhaps influenced by the success of the anthropological-zoological exhibitions that Carl

1 Jardin d'Acclimatation, Paris, 1999.

Hagenbeck Jr had been staging in the Hamburg Tierpark since 1874[3] – he presented a new kind of exhibition. This display, enclosed by a fence to protect the public, included not only African camels, giraffes, exotic species of cattle, elephants, rhinoceros and ostriches, but fourteen Africans ('Nubians') into the bargain. The addition of humans to the animal display was such a success that it was repeated in November of the same year, when six Greenland Eskimos were put on show. As Saint-Hilaire admitted, 'We recognize that we owe a very considerable portion of this augmentation [in the number of visitors] to the Nubians and the Eskimos. Given the costs and receipts, they pulled in a profit of 57,963 frs.' A record 985,000 visitors visited the Jardin in the following year (which coincided with the World's Fair) to see exhibitions of Lapps and Argentine Gauchos. Nubians were back on display in 1879. The yearly gate receipts dropped in 1880, a year in which no ethnographic exhibitions were held, but they rapidly picked up again in 1881, the year in which Eskimos and Fuegians (representing the extreme north and south of the Americas, respectively) were displayed there. By this time, a tramway had been constructed to the Jardin which made it even easier for large crowds – sometimes more than 50,000 a day – to flock to see the exhibitions. During the 1880s, their format became increasingly spectacular, focusing more on Africa as French involvement on that continent assured them of topicality.[4]

Another setting for these human shows besides the zoo was the theatre or music hall. For example, the Mapuche (Araucanians) from southern Chile who were on show in the Jardin in the summer of 1883 were regularly visited there by the French pretender to the Araucanian throne, Achille Laviarde (Achille I of Araucania from 1878 to 1902), who also introduced them to literary and political circles in the Chat Noir, a favourite cabaret of the French intellectual élite. Hence these human shows could play a role on the stage of international politics on occasion.[5] Across the border in the Belgian capital, where an unwritten law seems to have decreed that every *passage* had to have its own theatre, the Passage du Nord (today situated in the red-light district) had two: the Musée du Nord and the Musée Castan. The former, which opened in 1877, consisted of a show of waxworks and various theatres, including a Théâtre Bébé, where children and dwarfs put on farces and pantomimes, and a Salle des Fêtes, where variety shows were presented. The Musée Castan, founded in May 1888, followed the same pattern; in addition to a permanent show of waxworks, its Salle des Fêtes presented string puppets, exotic dancers, illusionists and other spectacles.[6] In February 1890, the Musée Castan hosted a short-lived presentation of Fuegians, immediately followed by the display of ten male Samoans, who played billiards and performed song-and-dance acts.[7]

Before looking in more detail at these human exhibits and the images to which they gave rise, it should be noted that we are not dealing with an exclusively European or colonial phenomenon. The urge to kidnap was already present on the very first day of Columbus's encounter with the New World. Describing his initial impressions of native Americans, Columbus concluded: 'To please Our Lord, I will bring six of them from here when I leave to Your Highnesses to learn to talk.' He immediately followed this statement with a comment on the lack of animals: 'I saw no animal of any kind, except parrots on this island.' These two sentences were logically connected in Columbus's mind: the native Americans formed a part of the natural history of the New World, on a par with its fauna.

It is not clear exactly how many people Columbus kidnapped during his first voyage, but the number of captives mentioned in his journal adds up to 31. The Italian humanist Peter Martyr – who must have met Columbus at the court of Queen Isabella – gave the figure of ten for those who set out for Spain, and three for those who arrived, 'the rest dying through adverse changes caused by the land, climate and food'. But although Europeans were already aware at this early date (Martyr's account circulated in manuscript form before its first printing in 1511) that a passage to Europe meant a passage to death for many, they carried on kidnapping and sending people. And although not every case of the display of humans was based on an act of kidnapping, in many cases it remains doubtful whether the human subjects participated voluntarily or not.[8]

As for the history of putting human beings on show, usually before a paying public, it can be documented in Europe into the twentieth century from as far back as the fifteenth.[9] Nor was it confined to Europe: in the Americas, the Aztec court of Motecuhzoma was no different, in that it contained a menagerie not only of animals and birds but also of albinos, dwarfs and hunchbacks.[10] At the other end of the chronological spectrum, the missionary Lucas Bridges, who grew up in Tierra del Fuego, records the participation of two or three Selk'nam (Ona) in an exhibition in Buenos Aires in the last decade of the nineteenth century.[11]

The particular history of kidnapping native Americans from the southern shores of South America began in 1520, when Ferdinand Magellan kidnapped two natives ('giants') of Patagonia to take them back to Spain. One of them died on the ship *Santo Antonio* 'when he felt the heat'; the other died of scurvy on Magalhães's own vessel.[12] The kidnapping of Fuegians got under way at the end of the sixteenth century, when in November 1599 Olivier van Noort, land-lord of the Double Keys tavern in Rotterdam, who had been put in charge of a joint Amsterdam-Rotterdam expedition organized by the Magellan Company to harass the Spaniards and Portuguese and to plunder the west coast of South America,[13] went ashore on the island of Santa Marta in the Strait of Magellan to hunt penguins. After killing all of the men and some of the women and children whom they encountered, the Dutch kidnapped the six remaining children (four boys and two girls) to take them back to the Netherlands. These Fuegians did not survive the voyage.[14] Another Dutch captain who was sailing in the same waters at the same time, Sebald de Weert, kidnapped a woman and her two children, whom he estimated to be four-and-a-half years and less than six months old respectively. The mother was put back on dry land with her baby two days later, but the eldest child was taken to Amsterdam and died there soon after-wards.[15] Cornelis de Pauw was later to cite the fact that she was only 137 cm tall as evidence that there were no giants in Patagonia.[16]

The best-known case, and the one that put the native peoples of Tierra del Fuego on the stage of European history, is that of the four captives taken by Captain Robert Fitz-Roy, commander of the *Beagle*, in 1830. Fitz-Roy's whaleboat was stolen. After weeks of fruitless pursuit of the real or alleged thieves, Fitz-Roy resigned himself to the loss of the boat, but not without taking captive four Fuegians: Yokcushlu, an eight-year-old girl of mixed Yahgan-Alakaluf parent-age, who was renamed Fuegia Basket; El'leparu, a young man, renamed York Minster; another youth, renamed Boat Memory by Fitz-Roy in memory of the whaleboat with which he was so obsessed; and Orurdelicone, a Yahgan taken from his family under false pretences by Fitz-Roy who entered history as Jemmy Button. Also on board the *Beagle* was the pickled corpse of a Fuegian which was later dissected at the Royal College of Surgeons.[17]

Boat Memory died within a few weeks of reaching England, but the other three were sent to a boarding school in Walthamstow. They were visited there by a variety of people and were introduced to the King at St James's Palace in 1831. They returned to Tierra del Fuego in December 1832 with the Second Surveying Expedition of HMS *Beagle*. One of those on board was the young Charles Darwin, who took advantage of the long voyage to get to know his Fuegian companions.[18]

Similar treatment was accorded the four Yahgan youths (including the son of Jemmy Button) from the mission station on Keppel (off the coast of the Falklands) who spent almost a year and a half in England between 1865 and 1867. Like their predecessors, they aroused the interest of aristocratic, missionary and scientific circles. Two of the four, Urupa and Jemmy Button's son, fell ill and died on the voyage back.

As we have seen, the settings into which native peoples of Tierra del Fuego were introduced on two occasions in the 1880s were very different. The Jardin d'Acclimatation, a place established to study the life, particularly the reproductive life, of exotic animals in a controlled setting, must have seemed an appropriate site for many to view a people widely regarded as little different, if at all, from animals. Charles Darwin stated: 'I could not have believed how wide was the difference between savage and civilised man: it is greater than between a wild and a domesticated animal,' and considered that 'the language of these people, according to our notions, scarcely deserves to be called articulate,' despite the fact that the Yamana-English dictionary compiled by Thomas Bridges (now in the British Museum) contained 32,000 words in the Yamana language.[19] The judgement of Johann Reinhold Forster, the naturalist who accompanied James Cook on his second voyage – 'Human nature appears no where in so debased and wretched a condition, as with these miserable, forlorn, and stupid creatures' – was echoed in Darwin's verdict:

These poor wretches were stunted in their growth, their hideous faces bedaubed with white paint, their skins filthy and greasy, their hair entangled, their voices discordant, and their gestures violent. Viewing such men, one can hardly make oneself believe that they are fellow-creatures, and inhabitants of the same world.[20]

Given this tendency to view the Fuegians as little more than animals, it is hardly surprising that, upon arrival in Europe, they were often treated as such. The menagerie of the Jardin d'Acclimatation, well on its way to becoming an entrepreneurial showplace by this time, was thus the spot to which eleven Fuegians (four men, four women and three young children) were taken and put on show in September 1881.[21] These Alakaluf had been kidnapped along the shore of the Strait of Magellan by a German sealer apparently acting on behalf of a German colonist active in the region, Johann Wilhelm Wahlen.[22] An attempt to kidnap six Fuegians by Wahlen on behalf of the Berlin Society for Anthropology, Ethnology and Prehistory in 1878 had been thwarted by the governor of Magallanes. Hagenbeck appears to have been behind this action.[23] A Captain Schweers took them via the French port of Le Havre to Hamburg, where they disembarked on 19 August 1881. From Hamburg, they were taken to Paris, the first stop on their tour.

Thanks to a contemporary engraving (illus. 2), we can gain some idea of what spectators paid to see. Fenced off from the public, a group of women and children are seated inside a hut made of leafy branches, the prominently displayed bones deliberately conjuring up visions of primitive cannibals. Behind them, a man is seated in a canoe, while a second group sits around a fire, holding tools or weapons. The engraving also shows various birds and animals within the precinct; besides serving to evoke a 'natural' setting, they are a reminder that the Fuegians were thought to occupy a rung on the ladder of civilization close to, or on a par with, dumb beasts. This juxtaposition of animal and (exotic) human themes can be found in the popular scientific publications of the period.[24] Local colour was heightened by the inclusion of authentic artefacts in the display, as the captain had brought a canoe, a bow and arrows and a few stone tools from the Strait of Magellan along with his human cargo.

The impression conveyed by an illustration is inevitably static. It is unclear exactly what the Fuegians were expected to do, and most of the written reports – as well as the sketches made by the artist Odilon Redon that are discussed below (see illus. 29–32) – stress their inactivity. They probably did little more than give demonstrations of their skill in shooting with a bow and arrow. Exotic people exhibited in the Jardin d'Acclimatation later in the 1880s, however, were expected to put on a much more spectacular display: they staged mock battles, did war dances, and performed feats on horseback and other circus activities.

Within a fortnight of the arrival of the eleven Alakaluf in France,

2 C. Nielsen, Fuegians in the Jardin d'Acclimatation, Paris, engraving from *Le Journal illustré*, 11 September 1881.

the young daughter of one of them (Petite-Mère) died. After being put on show in Paris for about three weeks, they were taken to Berlin, Leipzig, Munich, Stuttgart and Nürnberg. Their health was already beginning to deteriorate when they left Nürnberg in the wintry month of February 1882. One of the women died on the way to Zurich, and the health of the others was also poor by the time they reached Switzerland. Four of them died in Zurich, where the show was presented in the Plattengarten from 18 February to 23 March. At this point, Hagenbeck intervened and decided to send the five survivors home. One of them, Antonio, died on the voyage; only four of the original eleven managed to return to Punta Arenas (the sealer had given the governor there a bond as a guarantee of their return).[25]

Given the amount of travelling that the people on show had to do – nine Bella Coolas exhibited in Germany in 1885–6 were shown at more than twenty venues[26] – the long hours during which they were expected to appear to the public, and their exposure to European diseases, it is hardly surprising that mortality rates were high. Such high rates were characteristic of other human shows too: of the nine Aborigines taken from Australia by the showman R. A. Cunningham in 1883, only three were still alive at the end of 1885, when Prince Roland Bonaparte photographed them in Paris.[27] A revealing detail is provided by the fact that two of the Alakaluf who died in Zurich were found to be suffering from syphilis,[28] which they must have contracted in Europe. Given the strict supervision to which they were subjected, those responsible were most probably the guards, thus adding sexual abuse to the other humiliations to which the Fuegians were exposed.

The Musée Castan in Brussels was the setting for the presentation of a second group of Fuegians. Once again, there were eleven of them, but this time they were not Alakaluf (a canoe people from the western parts of the archipelago) but Selk'nam (also known as Ona), a land people who inhabited the interior of the main island and its northern and eastern coasts and who are now extinct. They had been captured on the Strait of Magellan by a Belgian whaler, who took them to Europe in chains 'like Bengalese tigers'.[29] They were displayed by the impresario Maurice Maître in Paris at the Exposition Universelle held to celebrate the centenary of the French Revolution – *liberté*, *égalité* and *fraternité* were clearly not extended to all. (Incidentally, the Chilean pavilion [illus. 3], made of iron, steel and zinc and specially designed for the Exposition by the French architect Henri Picq, was dismantled and taken to Chile in 1894 after it closed; having served for a while as the National Aeronautical Museum, it has been restored to its pristine state and now houses the Artequín museum of art replicas in the Quinta Normal de Agricultura in Santiago [illus. 4].)

In a photograph showing Maître beside the group (illus. 5), there are only nine; presumably, two of the original eleven had succumbed by the time the picture was taken. They were also put on show in London at the Westminster Aquarium, where they were presented as cannibals. For the price of one shilling, members of the public were admitted to see them fed on raw horse-meat.[30] After one of the women became ill, Maître abandoned her in London, where she died on 21 January 1890.[31] Maître had to flee with his remaining captives, taking them to Brussels. A contemporary daily newspaper reported:

A troupe of cannibals in Petits-Carmes – On Tuesday M. Le Jeune, Minister of Justice, ordered the arrest of the troupe of cannibals on exhibition in the Musée Castan. At present the unfortunate Ona are incarcerated in the Petits-Carmes prison as foreign subjects without means of support. The honourable Minister of Justice took this decision at the request of the British government. It appears that these Indians were captured in the British territories of Tierra del Fuego and forcibly taken on board a French vessel. One of them is even said to have been killed in an act of self-defence. The Indians were first exhibited in London. And the British police was going to investigate the facts concerning the capture of these poor people when they were dispatched to Brussels.[32]

3 Chilean pavilion at the Exposition Universelle, Paris, 1889.

4 Museo Artequín, Santiago, Chile.

5 The impresario Maurice Maître and a group of Selk'nam at the 1889 Exposition Universelle.

On the evidence of a member of the Société d'Anthropologie de Bruxelles who visited them in prison, there were seven of them by now (two fewer than the nine photographed in Paris, four less than the eleven who had originally been captured in Tierra del Fuego). These included a man of about 30 who had a slight beard, three women and three children, the oldest of whom was estimated to be about four years old. They had no tools or implements with them, though they would certainly have known how to use a bow and a lance. They were dressed in rags and walked barefoot in the snow.[33]

Maître was arrested in Brussels, and the survivors – certainly no more than four, and perhaps fewer – were returned via Dover and Liverpool on board the *Oruba* to Tierra del Fuego.[34] One of them, at any rate, José Luis Calafate, was still alive ten years later, according to the inscription on an anonymous photograph from 1899 (illus. 6).[35]

Besides the popular appeal of such exhibitions, they also attracted the interest of scientists. For instance, the anthropologist Franz Boas claimed to have received the impulse for his trip to the North-west Coast after having seen the Bella Coolas in Germany,[36] and the missionary ethnographer of Tierra del Fuego Martin Gusinde initially derived his interest in exotic peoples from the sight of Dinka and other Africans who were displayed in the streets of Breslau, as well as from the human exhibitions held at the Breslau Zoo.[37] Both of

6 Anonymous photograph with the following text: 'José L.M. Calafacte ten years after in the Salesian Mission of Río Grande, in 1899, Tierra del Fuego.'

the groups of Fuegians in England in 1831–2 and 1865–7 were examined by phrenologists. The presence of the Alakaluf Fuegians in the Jardin d'Acclimatation in 1881 was welcomed by the members of the Société d'Anthropologie of Paris as an opportunity to carry out measurements of all aspects of human anatomy. Léonce Manouvrier, a member of the Société, visited the exhibition five times in September 1881 and stated with satisfaction that he had been able to take no fewer than 50 measurements of each, though he complained that he had been unable to examine and measure the genitals. A colleague, Topinard, concentrated on the Fuegians' psychological and moral traits, while members of the Société d'Ethnographie focused on material culture and language.

The Société d'Anthropologie de Bruxelles likewise took a lively interest in the activities of the Musées in the Belgian capital. Its 1888–9 *Bulletin* contained a report by E. Houzé on some Hottentots who had been presented in the Musée du Nord, observing that 'it is a banal exhibition of no scientific value'.[38] Nevertheless, the next issue of the *Bulletin* contained a report of a lecture given by the same

29

E. Houzé on the group of Samoans who were being shown in the Musée Castan.[39] The haste with which the exhibition of Selk'nam in the same Musée was closed down meant that there was no time for the Société d'Anthropologie to visit the Samoans prior to their return to England. However, they were visited in prison by a member of the society, V. Jacques, who had hoped to organize a special session for the Société in the Musée du Nord before learning about their incarceration. Prison conditions prevented him from carrying out the measurements so dear to physical anthropologists of his time.[40]

'Fieldwork' conducted in this fashion was a lot easier than travelling all the way to Tierra del Fuego, though there were scientists who carried out work on the spot, such as Fernand Lahille from the Museo de la Plata, who took detailed measurements of several Selk'nam in Ushuaia in 1896 as well as photographing them,[41] or the members of the French Scientific Mission at Cape Horn (1882–3), who photographed and made plaster casts of the heads and bodies of the Yahgan who visited the base at Orange Bay, Hoste Island.[42]

In Paris, the gradual conversion of the exhibitions in the Jardin d'Acclimatation into a massive side-show eventually led to a rift with the Société d'Anthropologie. Some criticisms were of the virtually non-existent scientific value of the phenomenon – though it might provide a way to study physical characteristics, the detachment of the people on display from their natural environment meant that nothing could be learned about their social behaviour. Besides, the forced travellers through Europe gradually became acculturated, so that at least one member of the Société, Paul Nicole, could complain that the Fuegians on show in 1881 did not look like the people described in accounts he had read by travellers who had been there – a complaint that was echoed by the general public.

Criticisms of the human displays were prompted by humane motivations as well. Much has been written about the 'colonial gaze' and the power of colonial discourse as if they were monolithic phenomena, but the gaze to which the Fuegians and others were exposed was not homogeneous. The French captain Louis Martial, who saw two of the Alakaluf who had returned from Europe during a visit to Ushuaia in 1883, objected to 'the profane exhibition of the Alaculoofs in Paris' and promised to write against it when he returned to Paris. The shameful treatment of one of the eleven Selk'nam in London in 1889 who became ill and was abandoned to die there provoked an outcry in the press and on the part of the South America Missionary Society. Charles Letourneau, a member of the Société d'Anthropologie, described the Nubians displayed in 1879 as being 'set up at the Jardin d'Acclimatation a little like savage animals', and the almost clown-like presence of virtually nude natives of the Philippines displayed in the Parque del Buen Retiro in Madrid during the Exposición de Filipinas of 1897 provoked protests to the Spanish government on the part of Philippine students resident in the capital.[43] Lahille's sympathy for the Selk'nam he photographed emerges clearly from the following comment: 'The contraction in the features of some of the subjects … is due less to cold than to a certain apprehension caused by my camera (18x24) focused on them for the first time like an unknown weapon.'[44]

Visual representations of the Fuegians on show in Paris in 1881 began to circulate immediately. A number of photographs of them were taken by the commercial photographer Pierre Petit, who had obtained the exclusive rights to take photographs during the Exposition Universelle of 1867.[45] As his advertisement card (illus. 7) stated, Petit was the photographer of the French episcopate, of the Ministry of the Interior, of the Ministry of Public Instruction, of the Schools and Colleges of France, of the Faculty of Medicine and of the major learned societies of France. His photographs (illus. 8–12) show Fuegian males posing with weapons, while women are shown in proximity to children, against a background of branches. The latter evoke the hut, the 'primitive' home of the 'primitive family'. Moreover,

7 *Carte de visite* of Pierre Petit.

31

8 Photograph of Fuegians in the Jardin d'Acclimatation by Pierre Petit, 1881.

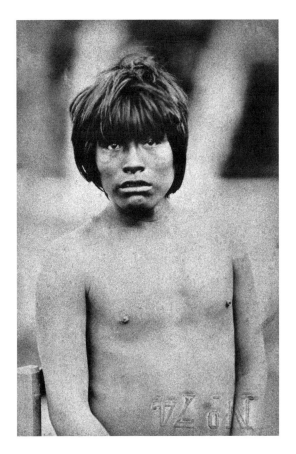

9 Photograph of Pedro, one of the
Fuegians in the Jardin
d'Acclimatation, by Petit, 1881.

10 Photograph of Fuegians in the Jardin d'Acclimatation by Petit, 1881.

11 Photograph of Fuegians in the Jardin d'Acclimatation by Petit, 1881.

there is nothing in these images to indicate that we are in fact dealing with Alakaluf, a canoe people whose subsistence was based on maritime resources, and not one of the terrestrial peoples like the Selk'nam. Two photographs by Petit (of Lise and of Petite-Mère and her daughter, which must have been taken a few days before the latter's death) were published together with a discussion in the *Bulletin de la Société d'Anthropologie* on 17 November 1881, and engravings after Petit's photographs were published in popular magazines, where the graphic illustrations ranged from scrupulous reproductions of the originals to generalized images in which the sitters' identities was lost.[46] An engraving in *L'Illustration* (illus. 13) closely follows the central group in one of Petit's photographs (compare illus. 8), while the central figure holding a spear was more freely adapted in Nielsen's engraving published in *Le Journal illustré* (see illus. 2). The version in *La Nature* takes stylization much further (illus. 14). The symmetrical display of accoutrements that frames the central scene

already betrays an eye that is more concerned with visual decoration
than with photographic verisimilitude; the man, woman and child
flanking the central scene were taken from one of Petit's photographs
(see illus. 10), but in the process the man's trousers held up by a belt
were replaced by a simpler, more 'primitive' self-supporting skirt, the
woman's breasts were reshaped, and the child shown shivering in the
photograph was given a fur wrap to keep it warm. Interestingly, the
central image includes Parisian onlookers, their 'civilized' dress and
manners pointing up the contrast with the 'primitive' Fuegians
huddled round the fire.

Photographs of a different kind were taken of the Fuegians by the
anthropologist Gustave Le Bon.[47] These adhered to the classic
anthropological convention of frontal and profile views advocated by
Roland Bonaparte and others[48] and lacked the contrived setting of
Petit's photographs. They were not taken against the conventional
background of a squared grid to facilitate anthropometrical study.

14 Fuegians in the Jardin d'Acclimatation, 1881, after a photograph by Petit, *La Nature*, 8 October 1881.

Instead, Le Bon affixed a graduated strip of paper to the arm of the subject for the same purpose.

A photograph of the impresario Maurice Maître with 'his' group of Selk'nam in front of a painted backcloth at the 1889 Exposition Universelle in Paris (see illus. 5) belongs to a different type: the self-presentation of the hunter with his trophy.[49] Photographs of this kind, like that of the Surinamese displayed at the Amsterdam World Exposition in 1883 (illus. 15), juxtapose European and non-European in an evident relation of hierarchy. Sometimes, this European presence could be felt to be an intrusion: two of the children in the Maître photograph are reproduced in an anonymous photograph now in Buenos Aires (illus. 16), but the European with his stick has been replaced by a tree to furnish a 'natural' setting for the Selk'nam boy. Such 'doctoring' of photographs often took place during the transition from photographic print to postcard: for instance, the civic buildings that form the background to Ojibwas in a canoe on the Thames in London in a collodium silver print of *circa* 1900 were replaced by a 'natural habitat' of rocks and trees in the postcard version of the same scene.[50]

15 Natives from Surinam at the World Exposition, Amsterdam, 1883.

As this Ojibwa example reveals, photographic representations of 'reality' are themselves artefacts that represent a construction within a specific frame. The emergence and development of photography did not mean a gradually closer approximation to reality, but the coexistence or succession over time of different 'realities'. In the case of the photographs of the Fuegians, there were as many versions of the sitters as there were photographers. The lives – and deaths – of those who were taken from their native Tierra del Fuego and brought to Europe are inevitably intertwined with the lives – including the disappearances and reappearances, flux and reflux – of their images. Moreover, since these photographs and engravings were not the first visual representations of Fuegians, it is worthwhile to see if we can trace any continuities in the mode of representation of these non-European peoples when seen through European eyes between the pre-photographic and photographic eras. For the photographs under discussion belong not only to the context of the photography of non-European subjects (so-called 'ethnographic' photography) but also to the longer history of European representations of the native peoples of Tierra del Fuego.

That history begins with the earliest allegory of America in the

37

sense of a representation of the continent by a female figure and her attributes.[51] It is to be found in an allegory of the five continents that forms the title page to the *Theatrum Orbis Terrarum* by Abraham Ortelius, first printed in 1570 (illus. 17). To the right of the personification of America, holding a club in one hand and a decapitated head in the other (following the image of America canonized in Cesare Ripa's illustrated *Iconologia* of 1603), we see a female bust surmounting a socle. Only the upper part of the body is shown because in 1570 only the northern (upper) part of the 'continent' below the Strait of Magellan had been discovered. The flames below the bust are an allusion to the name of Tierra del Fuego.

The earliest European visual representation of Patagonians is a copper engraving by Adriaen Collaert entitled *Americae Retectio* and produced around 1585 (illus. 18). This allegorical plate portrays the triumph of Magellan in discovering the strait that bears his name. Like Apollo Sol, the nude figure crowned with solar rays who is depicted guiding the boat, Magellan had circumnavigated the earth. The other mythological figures are Aeolus, sending a favourable wind from the clouds, two Nereids and a Siren holding the tip of her tail in one hand. But despite its mythological and allegorical content, the engraving is not devoid of any reference to American reality. In addition to the flames emerging from the landscape, two human figures, naked except for their skirts, are seen running in the distance behind a bearded giant wearing moccasins and a garland of foliage twisted around his waist; he holds a bow in one hand while with his other he thrusts an arrow down his throat. This may be a reference to the use of the arrow as an emetic described in the sixteenth century by Antonio Pigafetta as follows: 'When these giants have pain in the stomach, instead of taking medicine, they put down their throat an arrow two feet or thereabout in length, then they vomit of a green colour mingled with blood.'[52] Oral testimony credits Selk'nam shamans with the ability to pass arrows through their body without harming themselves.[53] The gigantic bird carrying an elephant, a clear reference to the mythological roc,[54] was also mentioned by Pigafetta, who reported that 'below Java the Great to the north, in the gulf of China ... is a very tall tree in which dwell birds, called Garuda, so large that they carry off an ox or an elephant from the place where the tree is'.[55] This engraving reached a wider audience, and thereby popularized this view of Tierra del Fuego, through its inclusion in the fourth volume of the *Great Voyages* published by Theodor de Bry in Frankfurt in 1593.

Three of the plates (after drawings by the surgeon Barent Jansz. Potgieter) published in the account of the Dutch expedition to the Strait of Magellan in 1598 under Jacques Mahu and Simon de Cordes

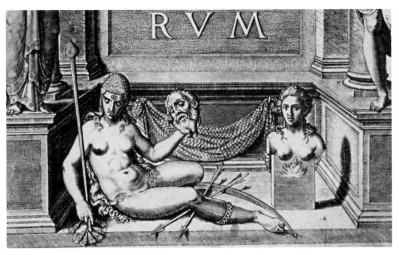

17 Allegorical title page showing 'America' and 'Tierra del Fuego', from A. Ortelius, *Theatrum Orbis Terrarum*, (1570) Antwerp.

18 Adriaen Collaert, *Americae Retectio, c.* 1585, copper engraving after a design by Jan van der Straet.

19 Natives of the Strait of Magellan, after a drawing in Barent Jansz. Potgieter, *Wijdtloopigh verhael van tgene de vijf schepen ...* (Amsterdam, 1600).

20 Natives of the Strait of Magellan, after a drawing in Potgieter, *Wijdtloopigh verhael van tgene de vijf schepen …*

21 Natives of the Strait of Magellan, after a drawing in Potgieter, *Wijdtloopigh verhael van tgene de vijf schepen …*

give some idea of what the native peoples inhabiting the Strait were supposed to look like at the time.[56] During an encounter with the Dutch in May 1599, the *Wilde* are described as between 3 and 3.5 m in height and exceptionally strong, in conformity with the mythical image of Tierra del Fuego as the land of giants. This is how the man and woman in the first plate appear (illus. 19); the (ethnographically accurate) fire in the canoe alludes to the name Tierra del Fuego. In the second plate (illus. 20), showing a woman and two children kidnapped by De Weert in December of the same year, they have been reduced to 'normal' proportions. The third plate (illus. 21) shows a female survivor of the massacre on the island of Santa Marta in November 1599. The representation of her male companion is supposed to have been based on the body of a male who was found dead there. Although the text refers to a feathered head-dress and feathered skirt on the man, the figure in the plate is in conformity with contemporary stereotypes of native Americans based on Brazilian dress.[57]

The work of European artists who relied heavily, though not entirely, on textual sources for their information, these early prints clearly tell us more about European conceptions of distant peoples and lands than about those peoples themselves.[58] However, the brief visits by Captain James Cook to Tierra del Fuego during his first and second voyages did result in the production of a number of on-the-spot representations. Moreover, some twenty objects acquired there during these voyages, of which only a dozen or so actually entered museum collections,[59] reinforced the importance of claims to verisimilitude by artists who had been there.

The in-situ representations made in 1769 by Alexander Buchan, one of the artists on board the *Endeavour* along with Sydney Parkinson, have been called 'models of documentary realism'.[60] A gouache on vellum, *A View of the 'ENDEAVOUR's Watering-place in the Bay of Good Success* (illus. 22), may be one of the first drawings 'in which an on the spot visual record was made by Europeans of their encounter with a non-European people at the time of the encounter'.[61] The small group of Fuegians (Haush)[62] shown are wearing cloaks made of animal skins, but no other information about their way of life is conveyed visually.

Two other gouaches by Buchan (illus. 23, 24), labelled as depicting a man and a woman from Tierra del Fuego – the latter is probably the same as the woman in a series of five drawings on one folio by Parkinson (illus. 25) – correspond in all essentials to the account recorded by Banks in his journal, so that the question of the mutual influence of

22 Alexander Buchan, *A View of the 'ENDEAVOUR's Watering-place in the Bay of Good Success*, 1769, gouache on vellum.

one source on the other arises. As for Buchan's pencil drawings (illus. 26), Smith suggests that, though presumably drawn on the spot, they may still betray the influence of earlier representations. So none of these images provide us with an unmediated picture of Fuegians.

Buchan's watercolour of inhabitants of Tierra del Fuego in their dwelling (illus. 27) shows a group of Haush sitting inside a hut, in front of which a fire is blazing. Skins are stretched on frames outside, and woven baskets can be seen hanging inside. The hut, constructed of leafy branches, corresponds closely to the version in pen and wash by Parkinson (illus. 28). This image was transformed in the hands of neo-classical engravers like Francisco Bartolozzi and eventually found its way into the published accounts of Cook's voyages.[63] What is interesting for our purposes, however, is to note the striking parallel between Buchan's representations of Fuegians in their hut in 1769 and the setting in which they were presented in the Jardin d'Acclimatation in 1881 (see illus. 2). And if Buchan's representation corroborated Cook's statement that the Fuegians were 'perhaps as miserable a set of People as are this day upon earth', the replication of that representation in the Jardin d'Acclimatation was bound to carry

23 Buchan, *A man of the Island of Terra del Fuego* [*sic*], 1769, gouache.

A MAN of the Island of TERRA DEL FUEGO.

24 Buchan, *A woman of the Island of Terra del Fuego* [*sic*], 1769, gouache.

A WOMAN of the Island of TERRA DEL FUEGO.

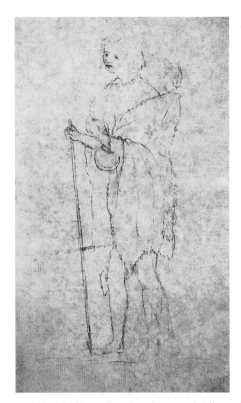

25 Sydney Parkinson, Drawing of a woman holding a stick and a basket with a child on her back, 1769, pencil.

26 Alexander Buchan, Two drawings of Fuegians, 1769, pencil.

the same message. Hence the 'evidence' provided by the Fuegians in Paris was used to support negative interpretations of Fuegian culture in works like Hovelacque's *Les Races humaines* (1882). Presentation, representation and interpretation were all caught up in a game of mutual self-reinforcement. What the eye saw was governed by what the mind thought; what the mind thought was dictated by the evidence of the senses …

Besides the visual representations considered so far of a more or less documentary kind, the Fuegians in Paris also aroused the interest of artists. The Parisian climate was ripe for them, as various presentations of native Americans during the previous decades had aroused a good deal of interest. The American artist George Catlin's Galerie Indienne, which presented images of Iowa and Chippewa in the rue Saint-Honoré from May to July 1845, was visited by Delacroix and George Sand in 1845; the latter recorded the power of the spectacle to 'passionner les artistes'.[64] When one of the group, O-Ke-We-Me,

INHABITANTS of the Island of TERRA·DEL FUEGO in their Hut.

27 Buchan, *Inhabitants of the Island of Terra [sic] del Fugeo in their Hut*, 1769, watercolour.

who had already lost a child in London, died on 12 June, she was given a funeral service and buried in Montmartre; Hippolyte Vattemare, Catlin's agent in France, proposed that a monument be erected in her memory. A collection was taken up among the circles of Romantic artists like Sand and Chopin, and the sculptor Auguste Préault was commissioned to design the monument in association with the architect J.-B. Lassus. A failure to raise sufficient funds prevented the monument from being realized, but among the parts that were completed is Préault's bronze bust of O-Ke-We-Me (now in the Musée des Beaux-Arts, Saint Lô), which was cast by Vittoz and exhibited for the first time in the 1849 Salon.[65] Though the bust's surface has deteriorated, the details of the long hair and shell necklace evoke something of the sentimental appeal that such figures held for artists of the time, and the fragmentary remains of the planned monument remind us that some Europeans at least were moved by the fate of the native Americans on show in the Old World.

Others drew on second-hand material instead of frequenting the actual presentations. Thus Gustave Moreau drew on magazines like *Le Magasin pittoresque* and *Le Tour du monde* for images of the non-European world. On one occasion, Moreau peopled a drawing entitled *Venus* with oriental types taken from the pages of these reviews to represent what he called 'les premiers hommes'[66] – an elision of the

28 Sydney Parkinson, *Natives of Terra [sic] del Fuego with their Hut*, 1769, pen and wash.

primitive and the primeval that he shared with many other artists, as well as with such writers as Gustave Flaubert. Though Moreau might be expected to have shown an interest in the Fuegians – he was a regular visitor to the natural history collections in Paris and was interested enough in the Hottentots to make a sketch of one of them, though not from life – there is no record of them in the collection of drawings housed in the Musée Gustave Moreau in Paris.[67]

As we have seen, one artist who did visit the exhibitions in the Jardin d'Acclimatation and make several sketches of the Fuegians was Odilon Redon (illus. 29–32). In his writings, his attitude towards them is mixed: while he admired what he interpreted as their pride and remarkable sangfroid, he saw them as representing a state barely above the animal and incapable of rising further.[68] In his drawings, however, he suggests their immobility by depicting the skins in which they wrapped themselves as solid and immovable; their heads emerge from these coverings as if from rocks.[69] Later *noirs* by Redon like *The Sphinx* (1883) and *The Idol* (*c.* 1886) continue the same association.[70]

Interest in the physiognomy of the Other was shared at this time by both physical anthropologists and their forensic colleagues. In 1881, the same year that Redon was sketching Fuegians in the Jardin, the sixth Impressionist exhibition included two pastels by Edgar Degas entitled *Criminal Physiognomy* and representing the teenage

29 Odilon Redon, Sketches of
the Fuegians in the Jardin
d'Acclimatation, Paris, 1881,
pencil on paper.

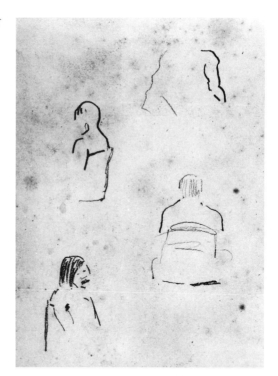

30 Redon, Sketches of the
Fuegians in the Jardin
d'Acclimatation 1881, pencil
on paper.

31 Redon, Sketches of the
Fuegians in the Jardin
d'Acclimatation, 1881, pencil
on paper.

32 Redon, Sketches of the
Fuegians in the Jardin
d'Acclimatation, 1881, pencil
on paper.

33 Eugenio Dittborn, *Histories of the Human Face VIII (The Scenario of the Sky)*,
Airmail Painting no. 78, 1990, paint, charcoal, stitching and photo-silkscreen on two
sections of non-woven fabric.

defendants in a recent murder trial. Six years after the publication of
Cesare Lombroso's *L'uomo delinquente*, non-European 'primitives'
and criminals were taken to be representatives of an atavistic past.

This combination of the criminal and the exotic resurfaced more
than a hundred years later in some of the *Airmail Paintings* by the
Chilean artist Eugenio Dittborn. In the series entitled *Histories of the
Human Face*, the faces of criminals are brought into contact with
faces drawn by the artist's seven-year-old daughter Margarita, and
with the faces of Fuegians taken from photographs (illus. 33). In this
crisis of faces coming together, Dittborn tapped on these representatives of outsiders (children, criminals, 'primitives') as icons in work
that was literally outside, for the *Airmail Paintings* – huge composi-
tions in which photographs and other graphic images were sewn
onto paper, folded and sent through the post in large envelopes – are
exhibited together with those envelopes. Each of them has thus
traced an intricate pattern of routes across continents. The *Remota*
exhibition of some of these works at the New Museum of Contemporary Art, New York, in 1997 and at the Museo de Bellas Artes,

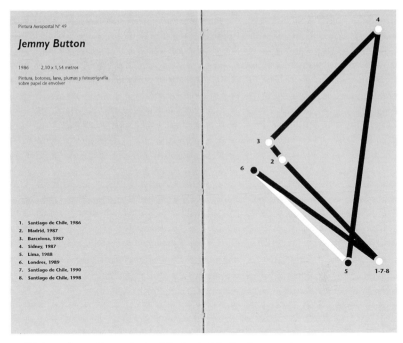

34 Dittborn, *Jemmy Button. Routes of the Aeropostales* (Santiago, 1997), p. 94.

Santiago, in the following year was accompanied by the publication not only of a catalogue but also of a booklet in which the abstract patterns traced in the air by these works were schematically represented, in transit (illus. 34).[71]

Like the Fuegians themselves, Dittborn's images have been caught up in an incessant movement between continents. What at first sight may look like a tasteless juxtaposition of images of Fuegians with portraits of criminals turns out to be true to their history. Other Latin American artists have also drawn on Fuegian iconography in recent years; for example, the Argentine artist Luis Fernando Benedit (1937–) has used visual material from Darwin and the missionary Lucas Bridges in installations created since the late 1980s.[72]

Images of Fuegians have been inserted time and again into widely different contexts.[73] This process of recontextualization is limitless, and the reactions it provokes can vary tremendously. When Captain W. Parker Snow met Jemmy Button in 1855, he showed him the drawings of himself and of the other Fuegians that had appeared in the second volume of Fitz-Roy's *Narrative* (illus. 35), provoking mixed reactions:

The portraits of himself and the other Fuegians made him laugh and look sad alternately, as the two characters he was represented in, savage and civi-

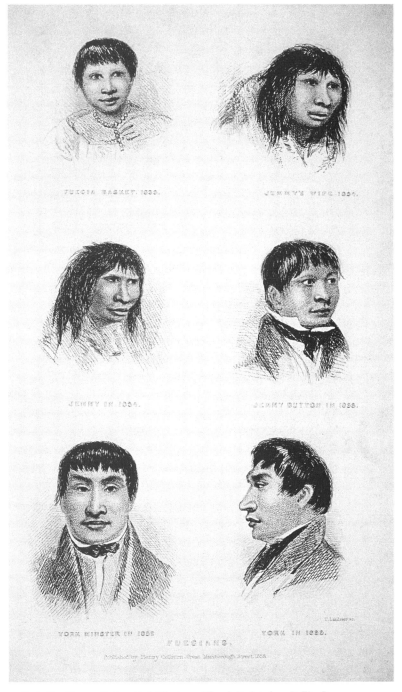

35 Portraits of Jemmy Button, York Minster and Fuegia Basket, from R. Fitz-Roy, *Narrative of the Surveying Voyages of his Majesty's ships 'Adventure' and 'Beagle'* … (London, 1839).

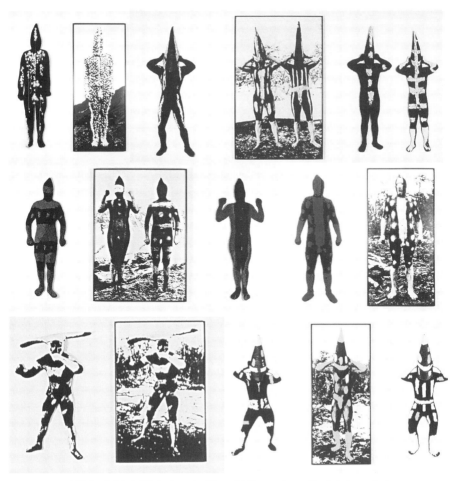

36 Elaine Reichek, Works from the *Tierra del Fuego* series, 1986–, knitting, painting, embroidered samplers, photographs.

lized, came fore his eyes. Perhaps he was calling to mind his combed hair, washed face, and dandy dress, with the polished boots it is said he so much delighted in; perhaps he was asking himself which, after all, was the best – the prim and starch, or the rough and shaggy. Which he thought, he did not choose to say; but which I inferred he thought was gathered from his refusal to go anywhere again with us.[74]

The installations from the series *Tierra del Fuego* (illus. 36) by New York artist Elaine Reichek reflect this mixed reaction. Reichek juxtaposed Selk'nam photographs by the ethnographer Martin Gusinde with knitted shapes of the same male figures stretched over armatures. The fact that these are *knitted* figures evokes the tragic role played by missionary donations of knitted clothing to the people of

Tierra del Fuego – the European germs brought by these clothes did more to wipe out the Fuegians than did the armed raids organized by the European settlers in the Southern Cone. By the turn of the century, the unrelenting epidemics, coupled with the lack of medical services and the destruction of the old way of life, had reduced the Yamana population from some three thousand to less than two hundred.[75]

In 2001, projections of Gusinde's photographs at larger-than-life scale at the multimedia *Cuerpos Pintados* exhibit in Santiago de Chile constituted yet another instance of the recontextualization of images of the Fuegians, this time in a display concentrated on body painting.[76] And of course, the inclusion of images of Fuegians in the present chapter is one more instance of their insertion within yet another context. Each of these contexts is at the same time a testimony to the power of images to speak in different ways to different audiences at different times in different places.

2 Being There

Not all of those who produced images of non-European peoples had the ability of an Odilon Redon. In fact, there was often an inverse correlation between documentary accuracy and artistic talent. For instance, the visual representations of native Americans by artists of the stature of Albrecht Dürer and Hans Burgkmair from the early sixteenth century betray a subservience to European canons of taste, a confusion of American and African physiognomy, and a greater familiarity with (Brazilian) artefacts than with their users.[1] On the other hand, the watercolours contained in two sixteenth-century manuscripts by the Dutch beachcomber Adriaen Coenen, including that of an Eskimo kidnapped in 1576 by Martin Frobisher (illus. 37) – the man was taken to London, where he died within two weeks – reveal a greater degree of documentary accuracy (the original may

37 Adriaen Coenen, *A curious history of a wild man and how he was captured and taken to London in the month of November*, 1578, watercolour from his *Visboeck*.

well have been a pamphlet by someone who had seen the Eskimo before his death), even though the style of their execution is as naïve as Coenen's style of writing.[2] The detailed watercolours illustrating American fauna, flora and people on the 134 leaves of the so-called Drake Manuscript, *Histoire naturelle des Indes*,[3] attributed to an anonymous French Huguenot who served under Sir Francis Drake in the last years of the sixteenth century, were executed in a similarly 'vernacular' style (illus. 38, 39).[4] If we move on to the seventeenth century, the eight full-length portraits in oils of different ethnic groups in Dutch Brazil by Albert Eckhout, which have been called 'the first convincing European paintings of Indian physiognomy and body build',[5] as well as the ethnographic drawings and paintings on paper attributed to him and now in Krakow – themselves images that have travelled over a remarkable trajectory – certainly betray the hand of an accomplished artist (illus. 40, 41).[6] However, the Krakow volume, known as the *Miscellanea Cleyeri*, also contains two pages of drawings of peoples of the Orient that were executed by a different artist in a much simpler style (illus. 42, 43).[7] Towards the end of the same century, a Dutch traveller to Sumatra who was also a competent amateur artist recorded lively scenes of smoking, dancing, milking and other everyday activities among the Khoikhoi at the Cape of Good Hope in 27 drawings on paper with a watermark datable to between 1688 and 1707.[8]

This tradition of what might be called vernacular portraiture of non-European peoples provides one of the contexts for a series of drawings of human figures from the Orient dating from the beginning of the eighteenth century. Among the collection of manuscripts of the Archbishop of Canterbury in Lambeth Palace Library, London, is a series of drawings of the inhabitants of Formosa, which to the best of my knowledge have never been reproduced in their entirety.[9] Six sheets contain a total of nine human figures. They are clearly related to the engravings of Formosans contained in George Psalmanaazaar's *An Historical and Geographical Description of Formosa, an Island subject to the Emperor of Japan, giving an Account of the Religion, customs, Manners &c. of the Inhabitants*, printed for Dan. Brown at the Black Swan, London, in 1704. The first step towards an evaluation of these images is therefore a comparison of the drawings with the engravings. However, since the latter are embedded in a description of Formosa, it is necessary to take the accompanying text into account as well. We therefore have three bodies of evidence – drawings, engravings, printed text – and thus the possibility of two kinds of discrepancy: discrepancies between drawing and engraving,

38 'Indian of Nicaragua', watercolour from *Histoire naturelle des Indes*.

39 'How the Indians usually have visions of the evil spirit', watercolour from *Histoire naturelle des Indes*.

40 Albert Eckhout (attr.), Negro girl, c. 1640, coloured-crayon sketch from *Libri Picturati A 38*.

41 Eckhout (attr.), A 'Tapuya' woman sleeping, drawing from *Libri Picturati A 38*.

42 Peoples of the East, from *Libri Picturati A 38.*

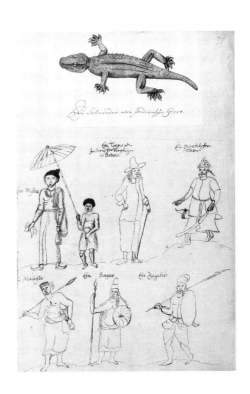

43 Peoples of the East, from *Libri Picturati A 38.*

and discrepancies between word and image.

The first image pasted into the Lambeth manuscript (illus. 44) is entitled 'Vice-Rex' and corresponds to the engraving 'The Viceroy' in the *Description* (illus. 45). There are minor differences between the two in the shape of the lance held in the Viceroy's right hand. That hand has five fingers plus a thumb in the drawing, while the engraving shows the correct number of digits. The more elaborate engraving depicts 'his Vest ... lin'd with the skin of some Tyger or Leopard',[10] a refinement that is absent from the drawing.

'Vice-Rex' is followed in the manuscript by a drawing labelled 'Civis' (illus. 46) which shows a bearded man smoking a pipe. If the object he holds in his left hand is a carafe, he is thus portrayed as the consumer of two kinds of stimulants. Attached to his belt is a circular plate to cover his genitals. To his left is a much smaller figure with a long stick (?) between his legs. The function of the latter, probably intended to represent the accoutrements of a 'Civis' (in other words, a burger) as a boy, is unclear (perhaps he is riding it like a hobbyhorse). Comparison with the engraving entitled 'A Burger' (illus. 47) shows a reversal of direction from the drawing. The engraved 'Burger' corresponds in most essentials to the drawn one, except that he is clean-shaven and the plate attached to his belt tapers to a point at the bottom. The details of the carafe and of the boy are absent.

The successor to the 'Civis' drawing is one of a 'Rusticus' (illus. 48), the 'Country Bumpkin' engraved on the same page of the *Description* as the 'Burger' (illus. 47). Both rustic figures wear the bearskin cloak mentioned in the text,[11] as well as a plate of brass, shells or bark to cover their genitals. The most salient differences between drawing and engraving are that the former includes some landscape details: a large and a small house, separated by a tree, and two plants in the foreground. All of these details are lacking in the engraving. The positions of the hands differ, in particular the fact that the 'Country Bumpkin' is smoking a pipe, unlike his drawn counterpart.

After the 'Rusticus' comes the 'Vice Regina' (illus. 49), corresponding to the engraving of 'The Viceroy's Lady' (illus. 50). The position in the drawing is shown in reverse in the engraving. The woman in the drawing holds two attributes – in her right hand what appears to be a flower, in her left a heart-shaped object (perhaps a purse) – neither of which is depicted in the engraving. Her costume in both representations, with its elaborate decoration of feathers, does not correspond to the text, which states: '... her Manto is made after the same fashion as the Queen's ... but that of the Vice-Roy's Queen

44 'Vice-Rex', 18th century,
drawing, Lambeth Palace Papers.

45 'The Viceroy', engraving from
George Psalmanaazaar, *An
Historical and Geographical
Description of Formosa* (London,
1704).

46 'Civis', 18th century, drawing, Lambeth Palace Papers.

47 'A Burger, A Country Bumpkin, A Virgin, A Bride', engraving from Psalmanaazaar, *An Historical and Geographical Description of Formosa …*

48, 49 'Rusticus' (left) and 'Vice Regina', 18th century, drawings, Lambeth Palace Papers.

50 'The Viceroy's Lady', engraving from Psalmanaazaar, *An Historical and Geographical Description of Formosa* …

is like a large Morning-Gown, which is worn here in England: Only it wants sleeves, and is lin'd with some Beautiful skin.'[12]

The fifth sheet in the manuscript contains four portraits (illus. 51). The 'Virgo inuxorata' and 'Sponsa' correspond to 'A Virgin' and 'A Bride' respectively (see illus. 47). The drawn 'Virgo' does not have a veil; she plucks a flower from a bush to her right. The engraved 'Virgin' is veiled, and her right hand is empty. The wide sleeves of the 'Virgo' are not found in the engraving, but we do find them in an engraving of a different woman, the 'Gentlewoman' (illus. 52). As for the 'Sponsa' and the 'Bride', while the former holds a flower in her left hand and a circular object in her right, the hands of the 'Bride' are empty. It is also noteworthy that the tall plumes surmounting her floral ruff are barely visible in the drawing. In this respect, the engraving is closer to the text, which mentions that the bride's head was adorned with flowers, laurels and feathers.[13]

A similar discrepancy between drawing and engraving can be found in the figure of the 'Vidua' on the manuscript's fifth sheet, corresponding to the engraving entitled 'A Widow' (illus. 53). While the woman in the drawing wears a flat-topped hat, the hat of her

51 'Virgo inuxorata, Sponsa, Uxorata, Vidua', 18th century, drawing, Lambeth Palace Papers.

52 'The Carillan or General, The General's Lady, A Gentleman, A Gentlewoman', engraving from Psalmanaazaar, *An Historical and Geographical Description of Formosa* …

53 'A Married Woman, A Gentleman's Nurse, A Widow, A Country-Woman', engraving from Psalmanaazaar, *An Historical and Geographical Description of Formosa* …

engraved counterpart rises to a point. The latter accords with the text: 'Widdows have another kind of a Cap which is twofold: The first which they put on their Head, is almost round like an English Woman's Coyff, the other is a little sharp-pointed.'[14]

The fourth figure on this sheet, 'Uxorata', corresponds to the engraved figure 'A Married Woman' (illus. 53). Once again, the engraved woman has a taller platter-shaped hat than her drawn counterpart. The latter holds a pail in her left hand and clasps what appears to be a hand in her right. The hands of the engraved 'Married Woman' are empty.

The final figure in the manuscript is the 'Rustica' (illus. 54), corresponding to the engraving entitled 'A Country-Woman' (see illus. 53). Like the 'Uxorata' in the drawing, she has what seems to be a hand in her right hand, while her left hand is concealed beneath her clothing. The woman in the engraving shields her breast with her left hand in a gesture of modesty. She is accompanied by a child, who is barefooted, in contradiction to the text, which states that 'they have shoes like their Mother.'[15]

While it is natural to suppose that the engravings were based on the drawings, it is hypothetically possible that the drawings were taken from the engravings. However, we can rule out this possibility for a number of reasons. First, as we have seen, the engraver tended to eliminate attributes from the drawings, leaving many of the figures empty-handed. The possibility that the draughtsman added those details on his own is unlikely. Second, in a number of cases the engraved figures are closer to the text than the drawings are. Note that all of the women in the engravings have necklaces, though this is not true of those in the drawings. The engraver was apparently following the text: '... all of them generally wear a Bracelet about their Arm; but the Women wear it both about their Arm and their Neck.'[16] This dependence on the printed text is particularly clear in the case of the only non-figural subject among the drawings, 'Tabernaculum in quo apparet Deus' (illus. 55), which is pasted into the manuscript in front of the 'Vice-Rex'. Many of the details of the drawing, such as the smoke emerging from chimneys or the idol of an ox-shaped deity, would be incomprehensible without explanatory material. The corresponding engraving of 'The Tabernacle and Altar' (illus. 56) follows the drawing, but it is inconceivable that the engraver could have created it on the basis of the drawing alone, as it clearly depends on additional information contained in the text of the *Description*. Third, the Lambeth catalogue's description of the drawings as 'rude' is no exaggeration. While the process of refinement as rude drawing was

54 'Rustica', 18th century,
drawing, Lambeth Palace
Papers.

55 'Tabernaculum in quo
apparet Deus', 18th
century, drawing,
Lambeth Palace Papers.

converted into engraving – a process that was extended further in later editions (illus. 57) – is quite understandable, the process of degradation implied by the reverse process seems implausible. For instance, it is easier to interpret the discrepancy in the number of digits on the right hand of the Viceroy – six in the drawing, five in the engraving – as a correction carried out by the engraver than to suppose that the draughtsman added an extra digit in the process of copying the figure from the engraving.

To these internal arguments we can add arguments of a different kind. On his own admission, when George Psalmanaazaar arrived in England he had little knowledge of English and wrote his *Description* in Latin. The use of Latin in the captions to the drawings would therefore imply that they predate the engravings with their English captions. We know from the minutes of a meeting of the Royal Society held in London on 11 August 1703 that Psalmanaazaar was present, so a date of October 1703 for the creation of the drawings, prior to the publication of the engravings based on them in April

57 'Le Roy', coloured engraving
from George Psalmanaazaar,
Description de l'Isle Formosa en Asie
(Amsterdam, 1708).

1704, yields a plausible chronology.

Who was the 'artist' of the drawings? It is hard to imagine that Psalmanaazaar would have contracted an artist with such a low level of skill to do the job for him. The supposition that the drawings are the work of Psalmanaazaar himself is borne out by the opinion of a handwriting expert who compared the writing of the Latin captions to the drawings with that of four autographed letters written by Psalmanaazaar and concluded that they were the product of the same hand.[17] In his later *Memoirs*, Psalmanaazaar mentions that, during a stay in Holland, he made 'a little book with figures of the sun, moon and stars' and other images.[18] Perhaps this was an earlier version of the drawings that were later worked up into the engravings. We may therefore concur with Foley that 'the Lambeth MSS … antedate the *Description of Formosa* into which they were later incorporated.'[19]

Although, as we have seen, there were 'vernacular' precedents for Psalmanaazaar's amateur portraits of non-Europeans, they cannot be regarded as models because they were not printed and therefore only circulated in manuscript form among a few hands. If we search for models on which Psalmanaazaar might have based his drawings, a number of visual parallels can be suggested. The presentation of the Formosans in pairs (king and queen, country bumpkin and country woman etc.) corresponds to common practice in the books of national costumes that began to circulate from the mid-sixteenth century.[20] In the case of the Formosan figures, it may be noted that the tendency of the engraver to remove details of landscape and distinctive attributes tended to flatten out the differences between the figures, rendering them more homogeneous like the pairs of figures in costume books. For the simple dress of the rural population, he could have drawn on a European tradition of representations of peoples from the primitive past of Europe itself or the primitive present of the non-European continents.[21] Contemporaries complained that the illustrations of Formosan dress were taken from the stage, and the costume of the 'Sponsa/Bride' in particular is reminiscent of the courtly masque. Other details, such as the various portraits of women carrying flowers, could derive from depictions of the peoples of the East such as those to be found in Jan Huyghen van Linschoten's *Itinerario* (1598).[22] What seems most unlikely is that Psalmanaazaar derived them all from the same source, or that he followed any particular model closely.

An Historical and Geographical Description of Formosa comprises three parts. The first is 'An Account of the Travels of Mr. George Psalmanaazaar, a Native of the Isle Formosa, thro' several parts of Europe'; the second is 'The Grounds of the Author's Conversion'; and the third is 'A Description of the Isle Formosa'.[23] This combination of an account of the author's travels with a description of the land(s) he visited is a commonplace in ethnographic literature from the sixteenth century to the present. For instance, Jean de Léry's illustrated account of the ten months he spent in Brazil (March 1557–January 1558) sandwiches a description of the country, its fauna, its flora and its inhabitants between one of Léry's outward and return journeys.[24] Psalmanaazaar's work shares the same structure. It is therefore worthwhile to examine what else his work has in common with the techniques of 'ethnographic' representation in both visual and textual terms.

One of these techniques is revealed if we return to some of the discrepancies between the drawings and the engravings. Take the flower held by the drawn 'Vice Regina' (see illus. 49) and that being plucked by the 'Virgo inuxorata' (see illus. 51). Neither flower appears in the corresponding engravings, but we do find one in the hand of the wife of the dignitary identified by Psalmanaazaar as the Carillan; she is labelled in the engraving as 'The General's Lady' (see illus. 52). Or take the engraving of the smoking 'Country Bumpkin' (see illus. 47). His drawn counterpart has no pipe (see illus. 48), but both the drawing (see illus. 46) and the engraving (see illus. 47) of the 'Civis/Burger' do. In these cases, an attribute appears to have been displaced or extended from one figure to another. Similarly, only one of the drawings – that of the 'Rusticus' (see illus. 48) – shows landscape features, including a couple of plants in the foreground; one of the engravings includes a plant in the foreground too, but it is not that of the 'Country Bumpkin' but that of 'The Queen'.[25] As we have seen, the disparities between the drawing and the engraving of the 'Virgo inuxorata'/'Virgin' imply a conflation between this figure and that of the 'Gentlewoman' (see illus. 52). In other words, in some cases the attributes which serve as identifying markers of specific ethnographic types who are clearly distinguished from one another in the printed text of the *Description* have either been suppressed or transferred to a different category. In a work that purports to enable the reader to gain an idea of the differences between certain human groups on the basis of observable characteristics, this refusal of the attributes to stay put thwarts any attempt at serious categorization.

Examples of this phenomenon can be found in the work of the first European artist to produce full-length ethnographic paintings, Albert Eckhout. Eckhout's large-scale portraits of four different categories of the population of Dutch Brazil in the seventeenth century, mentioned earlier, justifiably occupy a prominent position in the history of European ethnographic portraiture. Yet, as has been shown elsewhere,[26] characteristics of his earlier sketch of a black woman were distributed among a number of these paintings of distinct ethnographic types, not just to those with black subjects. We might be tempted to regard the way in which the engraver of the Formosan subjects transferred attributes from one category to another as carelessness, but if we bear precedents like that of Eckhout in mind, it is more appropriate to consider it as one characteristic of the exotic genre: non-specificity.

Such non-specificity also can be found in textual representations. This is the point, then, at which to widen the present inquiry to take the text of the *Description* into account, to see how it conforms to ethnographic practice. To begin with, the pages of ethnographic description cover an extremely wide variety of social facts. For instance, the Formosans had a sacred book, the work of a prophet called Zeroboabel, and they worshipped the sun, the moon and the stars as well as an ox. The *Description* includes an engraving of 'The Altars of the Sun, Moon and 10 Stars' that the citizens of every city on Formosa were ordered to build on a mountaintop.[27] The New Year's Day rite involved the decapitation of eighteen thousand boys under the age of nine and the offering of their hearts to the sun. The need to produce so many offspring for this sacrifice was the reason why the Formosans practised polygamy – though decapitation was the penalty for taking on more wives than one could afford to keep. They were also alleged to practise anthropophagy, a claim which Psalmanaazaar himself backed up by consuming raw meat in public. As for their language, Psalmanaazaar was no exception to the thirst for knowledge about primitive human language and script that was a preoccupation of many scholars in the seventeenth and eighteenth centuries. His audience, or at least its learned members, certainly were interested in the theories of the universal and ideal language planners, and he was bound to have taken this into account in providing an account of Formosan language and script.[28] These planners took a particular interest in reports of the languages of the New World and of China in the expectation that they might stumble across vestiges of an antediluvian, and therefore pure, form of language.[29] Attempts to devise 'real' characters were often based on Chinese models, and these efforts soon came to influence the literature of imaginary travel as well as more explicitly scientific treatises. An early example is Francis Godwin's *The Man in the Moon* (1638), which betrays the influence both of reports of spoken Chinese and of other details of Chinese ethnography derived from the diaries of Matteo Ricci.[30] Godwin also raised the possibility that the Amerindians might have migrated to Earth from the celestial spheres, thereby linking the 'savages' of the New World with extra-terrestrial aliens.[31] (Incidentally, if the date of composition of *The Man in the Moon* can be taken back to the 1590s,[32] the book can also be related to the intellectual turbulence occasioned by the travels of that period as reflected in *The Tempest* and in the work of John Donne.) In light of this background, Psalmanaazaar must have been aware of the demand for information about the language of Formosa. He certainly did not disappoint his readers, for the Lambeth manuscripts contain transcriptions of the Lord's Prayer and the Formosan alphabet (the translations are in Latin, but in other respects the transcriptions do not differ very much from those in the printed edition) complemented by 'native' versions of the Apostles' Creed and Ten Commandments.[33]

Many of the details of Psalmanaazaar's text are reminiscent of those reported for other cultures. The description of human sacrifices recalls the most notorious practitioners of such acts, the Aztecs. The Formosan punishment for murder, in which the condemned was hanged upside down for a period of time – a form of judicial punishment that can be documented everywhere in Europe, from Germany to Spain[34] – before being dispatched by a volley of arrows,[35] has a parallel in André Thevet's woodcut illustration (illus. 58) and account of the military aggressiveness of the South American Amazons:

They generally make war on certain other peoples and treat their prisoners of war in a very inhuman fashion. To kill them, they hang them by one leg from a high branch of a tree; and after leaving them for a while, when they return, if they have not yet expired, they shoot ten thousand arrows into them.[36]

Some aspects of Formosan religion, and the author's assumed name (borrowed from Shalmaneser, an Assyrian conqueror of the Israelites),[37] resemble Hebrew traditions. Certain details of vocabulary and the motif of the Trojan Horse evoke the Greco-Roman past. This evocation of antiquity was standard practice in ethnographic writing from the sixteenth century onwards. For instance, in writing *Les Singularitez de la France Antarctique*, Thevet had employed the Hellenist Mathurin Héret to bring out the parallels between the native peoples of America and the ancient Greeks,[38] but in fact this

58 'How the Amazons kill their prisoners of war', woodcut from André Thevet, *Les Singularitez de la France Antarctique* (Paris, 1557).

tendency could already be found in the earliest writings on the New World.[39] It was in conformity with the belief that one could 'read off' the practices of lesser-known peoples from those who were better documented. In this respect, Psalmanaazaar's account follows the same practice of writing ethnography as Joseph-François Lafitau was to follow in his *Moeurs des sauvages ameriquains comparées aux moeurs des premiers temps* (Paris, 1724).

Besides drawing on documentation on other cultures from the past, ethnographers were expected to compare their own experiences with those recorded in the accounts of other travellers. Psalmanaazaar's description of a chameleon, which he calls Varchiero – i.e., the Persecutor of Flies – is a borrowing of this kind, though his claim that the creature was only to be found in Formosa, Japan and America contradicts the sources.[40] Like many other travellers, he denied the existence of fabulous creatures such as dragons, unicorns and griffins.[41]

Another parallel between Psalmanaazaar's account and other ethnographies lies in the field of symbolic anthropology. On the basis of the engravings entitled 'A Temple' and 'The Tabernacle and Altar' in the *Description*, it is possible to deduce a system of symbolic classification in which masculinity, the east, the sacred, the right, the sun and superiority are the opposites of femininity, the west, the secular, the left, the moon and inferiority. As the anthropologist Rodney Needham has pointed out, such a system of analogic classification has world-wide distribution.[42]

There is a moralizing strain in Western ethnographies from the sixteenth century on. Thus the lesson that Michel de Montaigne and Jean de Léry drew from the Brazilian Indians was that the real cannibals were to be found among the usurers in the heart of Europe – who consumed their fellow beings in a long and drawn-out way – and among those who were prepared to kill in the name of Christianity.[43] Psalmanaazaar engages in similar moralizing in his discussion of the Formosans' dress:

The Formosans are certainly very curious in their Cloaths, but they affect no new fashions as the Europians do ... In this they excel the Europeans, that the Qualities and Conditions of Men may be discern'd there by the distinction of their Habits, whereas here a Nobleman cannot be known from a Tradesman by his Cloaths.[44]

The idea of using the exotic as a mirror of Europe persisted in the eighteenth century in Montesquieu's *Lettres persanes* and many other works of the Enlightenment. Psalmanaazaar formulated the rationale of his account of Formosa in similar terms: 'I supposed they were so little known by the generality of Europeans, that they were only looked upon, in the lump, to be Antipodes to them in almost every respect, as religion, manners, dress, etc.'[45] His moralizing extended to religion as well. The *Description*'s dedicatory epistle to Henry Compton, Bishop of London, has a strong anti-Jesuit tone. Certain details of the Formosan rite of child sacrifice deliberately carry the reader from Formosa to papist Europe to draw a parallel between Formosan cannibalism and the Catholic Eucharist.[46] The work's anti-Catholic tendency is explicit in the story of a Formosan priest who tricked a rich countryman into paying him huge sums of money to explain omens. When his deceit was exposed, the priest was imprisoned, but the countryman was executed for not having shown proper deference to him. The death sentence was pronounced by the Formosan high priest, who, Psalmanaazaar explained, was the equivalent of the Pope.[47] He made similar attacks on Catholic vows of celibacy and the contrast between fasting and feasting.[48]

Finally, a penchant for the exotic, or the tendency to heighten the exoticization of a subject, is revealed both in the text as a whole and in its details. For instance, the author gives a measurement of distance as twelve days' journey for an elephant before adding that this was the equivalent of six English miles.[49] The evocation of the non-European animal confers an exotic flavour on the method of calculation. In this respect, the material on child sacrifice and polygamy becomes nothing more than an extreme exoticizing response to the debate that was to persist throughout the eighteenth century regarding natural limits to population growth.[50] This tendency to exoticize went hand in hand with a relative lack of attention to ethnographic specificity. Aware that the farther removed the exotic locale was from the reader in space and time, the greater its credibility was,[51] Psalmanaazaar's account had to be exotic to be credible.

And credible it certainly was. On his arrival in England in 1703, Psalmanaazaar was presented to the Archbishop of Canterbury and, on several occasions, to the Royal Society. Following the publication of the *Description*, the author and his book became the talk of London. In the year after its publication, the patronage of Bishop Compton secured him a six-month stay in Christ Church, Oxford, no doubt in the hope that this would eventually further missionary activities in Formosa.

Not everyone was convinced, however. The astronomer Edmund Halley and the antiquarian John Woodward were particularly active in their attempts to expose Psalmanaazaar as an imposter. He responded with a 34-page preface to the second edition of the *Description*, published in 1705, in which he answered 'those Objections which the unmerciful Criticks have rais'd against me and the Book'.

But Halley, Woodward and the other critics were right. Psalmanaazaar had never been to Formosa. The account of his travels from there and through parts of Europe in the first part of the *Description* is a fabrication. That version of the author's life states that his contact with Europeans began in Formosa, where he received Latin lessons from a Jesuit from Avignon called Father de Rode. At the age of nineteen, after stealing gold and money from his father, Psalmanaazaar and his tutor left for Avignon via the Philippines, Goa and Gibraltar. After being threatened by the Inquisition in Avignon, Psalmanaazaar claimed to have made his escape by bribing a sentinel and travelling along the Rhône into Germany, where he was press-ganged into the Elector of Cologne's army. Having been released from military service because of his religion, on arriving in Cologne he was recruited again. The army's movements took him to 's-Herto-genbosch and, finally, to Sluis in Flanders, where he met up with a Reverend Innes and was converted to the Church of England (the account of his travels is followed by a lengthy exposition of 'The Grounds of the Author's Conversion').

In fact, Psalmanaazaar wrote two accounts of his life: the one in the *Description*, and a second version contained in his *Memoirs*, written in the 1720s and published posthumously in 1764. In the latter, he states categorically: 'Out of Europe I was not born, nor educated, nor ever travelled.'[52] Though he refuses to reveal his name or nationality, the man who assumed the name of George Psalmanaazaar (he later dropped the double 'aa' to make it Psalmanazar) was probably born in the south of France in or soon after 1679. After his family had come down in the world and he had been reduced to begging, he started to pass himself off as a persecuted Irish Catholic, forging a counterfeit pass to that end. Recruited into a regiment in the pay of the Dutch, he hit on the idea of passing himself off as a Japanese and behaved in a correspondingly outlandish way. It was during his stay in Holland that he tried his hand not only at impersonating but also at producing written fabrications when he made 'a little book with figures of the sun, moon and stars, and such other imagery as my phrensy [*sic*] suggested to me, and filled the rest with a kind of gibberish prose and verse'.[53] At some point, he was introduced to a Reverend Alexander Innes,[54] a chaplain attached to the troops in Flanders, who is credited with having seen how the young man's remarkable linguistic and mnemonic talent could be turned to financial and social advantage. Benefiting from the gap in reliable knowledge about Formosa before

76

the middle of the eighteenth century, Psalmanaazaar was taken to London by Innes and assumed the guise of a Formosan native; this was the point at which, to add credibility to his story, he consumed raw meat in public.

Both accounts are full of disguises and counterfeits. Father de Rode was only able to operate in Formosa by disguising the fact that he was a Jesuit and assuming a false personality. Psalmanaazaar operated for a while with a false pass, and eventually had difficulties in changing that pass from an Irish to a Japanese one because of what he called his 'indifferent' hand[55] (an epithet equally applicable to his artistic skill, or lack of it). Though the later account is presented as the whole truth written by a repentant sinner (albeit one high on laudanum at the time!),[56] there is no reason to suppose that it does not contain fabrications.[57] In fact, we are better informed from contemporary sources about his later life. Although his deceit was never unmasked definitively, he withdrew from public notice after a few years and ended up as a hack writer. He was a close friend of Samuel Johnson, who called him 'the best man he had ever known'.[58]

Writing at a time when the responsibilities of authorship were in a state of upheaval and when conventions of originality, genius, authenticity, documentation and so on were in a state of flux, Psalmanaazaar had an undeniable flair for producing a strong sense of authenticity,[59] which he used skilfully to write an ethnography that could convey such a degree of conviction that it was not at once seen to be a fabrication. Psalmanaazaar was well aware that he was treading on thin ice. By deliberately contradicting the reports on the Far East by Varenius and others with which Reverend Innes supplied him, Psalmanaazaar boldly used his divergence from them as proof of the authenticity of his own, even inventing an imaginary Franciscan missionary, Prince Albert Lubomirski, to give credence to his obvious errors.[60] The ruse of recognition by which the exotic could be used to terrorize authority had to produce a sufficient degree of difference from other accounts to make the author's position credible, while not going too far beyond a system of analogies to make his account incomprehensible.[61] Besides, earlier accounts of Formosa were not much better, and at some points both the Dutch missionary Candidius and the Jesuit Du Halde indulged in fantasy just as much as Psalmanaazaar did.[62]

Psalmanaazaar's *Description* belongs to a variety of contexts. It featured in an exhibition on fakes in the British Museum in 1990,[63] and, as the product of a liar, it clearly has a place in the history of literary forgeries.[64] If 'the distinguishing mark of the period between

1750 and 1850 – in England at any rate – would be not the new professional practice of history but the increasingly expert production of
pseudo-historical forgeries',[65] the *Description* can be regarded as an
early example of such a forgery. Its fantastic and picaresque travel
account make it a precursor of *Gulliver's Travels* and *Robinson
Crusoe*,[66] as well as of later literary creations like Frederic Prokosch's
The Asiatics (first published in 1935), which was widely acclaimed for
its accurate depiction of exotic places and peoples, even though
Prokosch (1908–1988), whose activities including forging first
editions of works by Yeats, Eliot and other modern writers, had never
been to any of the countries he described. The *Description* also continued to have an influence on missionary activities: Psalmanaazaar's
Dialogue between a Japonese and a Formosan, a pamphlet he published
in 1707 that purported to document a dispute between pagans about
their religious views and beliefs, was still being reprinted in 1896 as a
contribution to the missionary effort in Formosa because of 'its interest at a time when the Japanese are brought, unexpectedly and in a
very real sense, face to face with the hill tribes of Formosa'.[67]

One of the purposes of this chapter has been to show how
Psalmanaazaar's images of Formosans belong to the history of the
'vernacular' portrayal of non-Europeans – a history, by the way, which
still continues.[68] Unlike the images of Fuegians discussed in Chapter 1,
where the itineraries of images on the move were shown to be intertwined with the movement of people themselves, Psalmanaazaar's
images of Formosans were produced in London by a man who, on his
own admission, had never been out of Europe. The verisimilitude of
such creations derives from their conformity to the implicit rules and
practice of ethnographic representation, not from their correspondence to objects and practices encountered in the field.

Finally, there is another context into which Psalmanaazaar's work
can be inserted: the 'para-ethnographic' one. While imprisoned in the
Bastille a year before the outbreak of the French Revolution, the
Marquis de Sade wrote a 'roman philosophique', *Aline et Valcour*, in
which the travels of Sainville and Léonore, two lovers who become
separated, are described at length. Sainville's shipwreck off the coast
of Africa provided Sade with an excuse to dwell on the cruel practices
of the cannibal Jagas and Butua. But there was no need for the
Marquis to invent horrific forms of torture – he drew many of them
from ethnographic compendia at his disposal in what was virtually
the 'University of the Bastille' at that time.[69] Another example of this
embedding of ethnographic details within a fictional text is *Iolāni; or
Tahiti as it was. A Romance*, Wilkie Collins's earliest novel, which was

turned down by two publishers because of scenes in which the author's youthful imagination ran riot among noble savages (it was only published for the first time in 1999). *Ioláni* is a tale of infanticide, human sacrifice and sorcery set in Tahiti prior to European contact. Yet, though the inclusion of the word *romance* in the title makes it clear that it is a work of fiction, among the sources on which Collins drew was *Polynesian Researches* by William Ellis of the London Missionary Society. Collins even incorporated Ellis's explanation of the sound of Polynesian vowels into a note to the manuscript. The author's confinement to the desk of a London tea-trading company at the time must have been as irksome to him as confinement in the Bastille was to De Sade; both writers resorted to the same expedient of drawing on explicitly nonfictional material as a substitute for first-hand observation.[70]

Psalmanaazaar's *Description* is a work of fiction that was presented as ethnographic fact; novels like *Aline et Valcour* or *Ioláni* offer ethno-graphic facts embedded within texts that present themselves as works of fiction. In both cases, we are faced with works that, although they do not conform to the norms of canonical ethnography, cannot be cleanly separated from it either. And it is their very hybrid form of existence as 'para-ethnography' which makes it impossible to demar-cate the boundaries of a canon or corpus.

3 From America to Oxfordshire?

One of the lessons we can draw from the difficulty of pinning down Psalmanaazaar's Formosans to a single context – the resistance of the hybrid to being classified as fiction or nonfiction – is the need for a *historical* iconography and anthropology that take into account the fact that the constitution of a distinction like that between fact and fiction, or between the imaginary and the non-imaginary, has its own history. In fact, these are historical categories. In 1976, for example, William Sturtevant compiled a useful list of 268 depictions of native Americans down to 1590, deliberately confining his catalogue to illustrations 'having some claim to ethnographic accuracy'.[1] But a *historical* iconography requires us also to take into account those illustrations that were presented *at the time* as representations of native Americans, irrespective of whether they conform to our own standards of fact and fiction. Hence Sturtevant's claim that 'When one subtracts from European pictures the elements anthropologists can verify as authentically Indian, what remains are European preconceptions and misconceptions'[2] betrays a positivism that is out of place in the study of the lives of images, for their very vitality enables them to pass from one context to another.

Another distinction that is irrelevant for our purposes is that between human and animal. In Chapter 2, we came across figures of native Americans in the Drake Manuscript, a work that presents itself as a natural history (its full title is *Histoire Naturelle des Indes: contenant Les Arbres, Plantes, Fruits, Animaux, Coquillages, Reptiles, Insectes, Oyseaux, &c. qui se trouvent dans les Indes; Représentés Par des Figures peintes en couleur naturelle; comme aussi les diférentes manières de vivre des Indies; Savoir: La Chasse, La Pêche, &c. Avec Des Explications historiques*). What are human beings doing in a work of natural history? The Drake Manuscript is not exceptional in this respect; the chronicler Gonzalo Fernández de Oviedo y Valdés, who spent approximately 30 years in the New World, prepared at least twenty ethnographic illustrations relating to Hispaniola, Central America,

Peru and Patagonia which found their way into the various editions of his publications under the rubric of 'historia natural'.[3] A combination of human, plant and animal subjects can be found in the illustrations to the works of André Thevet, cosmographer to four French monarchs, even if the focus on the documentary portrayal of Brazilian plants and animals in his *Singularitez de la France Antarctique* (1557) becomes subordinated to scenes of human activity in his *Cosmographie universelle* (1575).[4] The presentation of human beings in the Jardin d'Acclimatation and other menageries (see Chapter 1) shows that this inclusion of non-Europeans within the world of natural history was still operating in the nineteenth century. Consequently, one of the problems facing anyone setting out to trace the lives of images of non-European human subjects is: how does one know where to look?

A second issue is the problem of origins, in particular the question of the first image. In theory, there exists a first image of every New World phenomenon that entered the field of European representations. Since in the sixteenth century 'America and, more generally, the distant lands, were above all vast repositories of animals, plants and minerals waiting to be known and classified,[5] this implied an equally vast series of *primeurs* – the first image of an American armadillo;[6] the first image of a colibri (1519; Raphael's Vatican Loggias);[7] the first image of a llama (1530; woodcut in Lorenz Fries, *Underweisung und uzlegung Der Cartha Marina*);[8] the first image of a sloth (1557; woodcut in Thevet, *Les Singularitez de la France Antarctique*);[9] the first image of a potato plant (1588; watercolour in the collection of Charles de l'Ecluse);[10] the first image of a Brazilian tortoise, the *Testudo denticulata* (c. 1640, oil painting on paper attributed to Albert Eckhout);[11] and so on. And since human beings formed a part of the world of natural history at this time, it also implied the existence of first images of human figures – the first image purporting to be of native Indians (woodcut frontispiece to Giuliano di Domenico Dati's version of Columbus's *La lettera dell isole che ha trovato nuovamente il Re di Spagna* in *ottava rima*, printed in 1493);[12] what Sturtevant has called 'the earliest illustration meriting serious attention' (woodcut of *The People of the Islands Recently Discovered* dating from 1505);[13] the earliest painting of native Americans (some have argued that it is Jan Mostaert's *West Indian Landscape*; see below); the first full-length paintings of native Americans in European art (Eckhout's paintings of Brazilian subjects in the 1640s);[14] the first three-dimensional European representation of native Americans (the subject of this chapter); and so on. In other words, the question 'Where to start?' seems to have an easy answer: 'With the first European images to be produced after Columbus's "discovery" of America in 1492'.

However, the historian Marc Bloch's warnings about what he called 'the idol of origins',[15] as well as the need to distinguish between origin and genesis,[16] should serve to put us on our guard. For the lives of images of America date from before 1492, both in the European imaginary and on the American continent itself. I shall demonstrate this by following sixteenth-century practice and setting the analysis of representations of human figures within the wider context of natural-historical illustration.

The American turkey, a member of the pheasant family (*Meleagris gallopavo*), is native to Central and Southern America. The conquistadors brought it to Europe in the 1520s, shortly after introducing the African guinea-fowl (*Numida meleagris*) to the New World – a crisscross movement which probably goes a long way to explaining the subsequent terminological confusion between the two.[17] It is not clear whether the turkey was among the exotic animals that Dürer saw in Brussels in 1520 (it is not included in his sketches). At any rate, a reference to an *indianisch han* in Nürnberg in 1531, followed by its inclusion in Rabelais' *Gargantua* three years later, indicates that the New World turkey reached Northern Europe at some point in the second decade of the sixteenth century.[18]

When was the European image of the American turkey born? In the most detailed study of the iconography of the turkey to date, Lise Lotte Möller remarks that it took some time for the turkey to feel at home in the visual and textual record.[19] The earliest European illustration to which she refers is from a fresco entitled *L'Ignorance chassée*, executed in the decorative style of the School of Fontainebleau between 1534 and 1537, though the argument is based on a restoration carried out in the 1960s. If this turkey is authentic, it must have been an emblem for stupidity.[20]

The earliest extant example, which apparently escaped Möller's keen eye, is the turkey which makes its inconspicuous introduction in the company of a dove, a peacock and an equally exotic bird of paradise on the carved wooden border of a backgammon board signed by Hans Kels the Elder and dated 1537 (Kunsthistorisches Museum, Vienna). The horizontal parts of the border are decorated with animals, while the vertical parts are decorated with birds. Most of the sixteen *tondi* which divide these animal sections, and the 30 playing counters, are decorated with scenes from Ovid's *Metamorphoses*. It is assumed that both board and pieces were made for Emperor Ferdinand I (1503–1564), about whose collections little is known, and that the artist should be sought in Augsburg in the work-shop of Jörg Breu the Elder (*c.* 1475–1537) or of his son of the same name (*c.* 1510–1547).[21]

The turkey reappears in the work of an artist who was also associ-ated with Fontainebleau, this time in an ornamental cartouche after Léonard Thiry (illus. 59), which must have been designed before his death in 1550.[22] The cartouche with the turkey also includes a woman holding an arrow, a winged nude with a quiver, a cat, a dog, a chicken and a snail. The scene inside the cartouche is of Medea performing an animal sacrifice at the altars of Hades and Youth under the eyes of Proserpina and Pluto.

Another early setting for the American turkey, also dating from the 1540s, is the pergola in the Villa Giulia in Rome, painted by Pietro Venale and his assistants.[23] Particularly influential in this instance were the woodcut in Pierre Belon's *L'histoire de la nature des oyseaux* (illus. 60),[24] and the turkey in Conrad Gesner's *De avium natura* of the same year (1555). In the plastic arts, Giambologna's 62-cm-tall bronze turkey made for the Grotto at the Villa Medici, Castello (together with a pigeon, a thrush, a falcon, an eagle, an owl and possi-bly a peacock) in 1567 was probably the model for a silver German perfume flask from the second half of the sixteenth century.[25] Nor

59 René Boyvin, Engraving after a design by Léonard Thiry from a series of prints for *Livre de la Conqueste de la Toison d'Or* (Paris, 1563).

60 Pierre Goudet, Woodcut from Pierre Belon, *L'histoire de la nature des oyseaux* (Paris, 1555).

should we overlook the turkey that appears, among other Americana, in a series of tapestries in Wawel Castle, Krakow, after cartoons by an anonymous artist from Antwerp, presumably from the circle of Pieter Coecke van Aalst, completed for Sigismund II Augustus before 1565.[26] Thus illustrated works of natural history, the decorations of villas, mythological works, royal arrases, grottoes and *Kunstkammer* objects are among the contexts into which the image of the American turkey was inserted.[27] Whether we are talking about the exotic contents of the Renaissance *Kunst- und Wunderkammern*, to which the backgammon board belongs, or the equally exotic contents of the Fontainebleau grotesques – both hardly contexts characterized by realism – the creature itself is portrayed realistically enough to make it possible to identify.

European artists did not always come up with convincing, or even clearly identifiable, representations of New World animals. There is a passable image of a llama in the 1530 woodcut mentioned above, but the less llama-like a creature looks, the harder it is to make the identification. For example, in a print by Etienne Delaune (*c.* 1518–1583) of one of the four continents known at the time, unmistakably identified by the name 'Americca' and dated 1575 (illus. 61), we see a naked

AMERICCA   1575 . S F .

61 Etienne Delaune, *Americca*, 1575, engraving.

female figure wearing an armband and feathered head-dress, armed with a bow and arrows and seated in front of a creature that has been identified as a llama. The art historian S. Poeschel, on the other hand, has refused to accept this identification; in her eyes, this is a fabulous creature, like the dragon in Delaune's allegory of Africa. A. Wendt also has had difficulties in accepting the identification as a llama because the creature carries its young in a pouch like a kangaroo.[28] And what are we to make of the scaly creature in the background to a personification of America on a German lead plaquette (illus. 62)? It is clearly based on Dürer's famous rhinoceros, but did the rhinoceros serve as a model for another scaly animal which the artist had never seen but whose description sounded remarkably similar: the giant armadillo?[29]

The turkey, despite its realism, appears in the contexts enumerated above in conjunction with blatantly mythological creatures, including, on the backgammon board, a griffin, a phoenix and a winged nude. In other words, the distinction between myth and reality does not seem to be pertinent here. It is also worth noting that, although the turkey appears in the vicinity of narrative scenes, it bears no relation to them. On the backgammon board, it appears between the scene of Circe transforming the companions of Odysseus into swine and that of Jupiter's adultery with Antiope. In the case of Thiry's

85

62 Personification of America, *c*. 1580–90, lead plaquette with traces of gilt.

cartouche, the turkey is part of the frame around a scene taken from the Greek myth of Jason and the Golden Fleece.[30] In neither case does the bird have anything to do with the scenes in question. This phenomenon is by no means confined to the turkey. For instance, while the ceiling of the Uffizi armoury in Florence painted by Ludovico Buti in 1588 contains accurate depictions of birds from Central and South America, they share the same pictorial space as fantastic mythological creatures.[31]

These first European images of the turkey are not the first images of the bird. Pre-conquest Mesoamerican codices contained images of native birds, animals and plants. The turkey (*chalchiuhtotolin*) appears, for example, in the *Codex Fejérvàry-Mayer* and *Codex Laud* (illus. 63, 64). These two codices (from the so-called Borgia group) date from the pre-Hispanic era.[32] Indeed, it would be hard to imagine that representations of a creature like the turkey, which had been

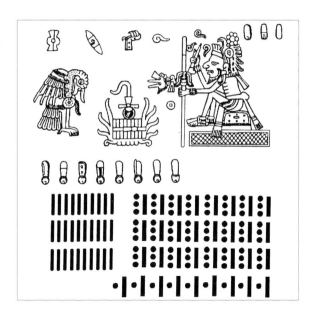

63 A turkey in a sacrificial scene, from the pre-Columbian *Codex Fejérvàry-Mayer*, pigment on deerskin.

64 Turkey, from the pre-Columbian *Codex Laud*, pigment on deerskin.

domesticated long before the conquest, would not be found in pre-conquest artistic traditions. The same is true of the colibri: although the first European image dates from 1519, the creature can be found in the *Codex Borgia* (*quetzalhuitzilin*) and *Codex Laud* (illus. 65, 66), as well as among the geoglyphs of the famous Nasca Lines and in Nasca ceramics and textiles from the beginning of the Christian era.[33] This bird played an important role in both Andean and Mesoamerican

65 Colibri, from the pre-Columbian *Codex Borgia*, pigment on deerskin.

66 Colibri, from *Codex Laud*, pigment on deerskin.

mythology, and was one of the avatars of Huitzilopochtli, the national god of the Aztecs.

Paradoxical though it may sound, there are pre-1492 European images of America too. By this I mean that there is a striking continuity between the tendency to portray unfamiliar peoples in terms of a stock of figures – the so-called 'Plinian' monstrous human races (though some of them go back centuries before Pliny) to which Wittkower devoted his seminal 1942 article – on the one hand,[34] and the use of the same images to represent native Americans, on the other. The 1530 woodcut of a llama already provides us with an example, for the scene in question is peopled by the dog-headed creatures known in the literature as Kynokephaloi (illus. 67),[35] who were assumed by Columbus and others to have peopled parts of South America.[36] In fact, at least some of the Plinian races were known in the Mexican court before the conquest.[37]

67 Dog-headed and human-headed hybrid, woodcut from Hartmann Schedel, *Liber chronicorum* (Nürnberg, 1493).

Just as European artists often failed to produce a representation of a New World animal that could be identified without difficulty, so – with the exception of Christoph Weiditz's eleven drawings of Aztecs made in 1529 – did their renderings of physiognomy and physique have little American about them.[38] Artists like Dürer and Burgkmair had never been to the Americas, nor had they had much opportunity to see the native Americans who were brought to Europe at various points in the sixteenth century. Inevitably, if they did not have recourse to the stock of monstrous images to portray those peoples who fell outside the limits of European civilization, they fell back on classical canons for representing the human figure. Among the very earliest visual sources on the Americas, the marginal sketches to the compilation of sailors' reports and original official sources on the discovery of the New World by Alessandro Zorzi, we find 'two images of gold' depicted as Renaissance statues, and the text on young men 'of fine stature' illustrated by equally statuesque Renaissance figures.[39] The classical *contrapposto* pose characterizes what has been taken to be a native of Brazil in a marginal illustration by Dürer to

Emperor Maximilian's *Book of Hours* of 1515 as a visual comment on Psalm 24: 'The earth is the Lord's and the fullness thereof.' The human figure in question, however, has no native American features.[40] Similarly, the British Museum holds two drawings attributed to Burgkmair of a figure associated with what are presumed to be native American attributes – a Mexican shield, what may be a Mexican club and a Brazilian head-dress apparently worn back to front – but the physiognomy is distinctly negroid.[41] In other words, while natural-historical criteria were by and large adequate to identify distinctly American flora and fauna, they were inadequate when it came to identifying native Americans. At this point, culture took over where nature left off: if natural distinctions were hard to draw, human beings would have to be identified as native Americans by means of cultural attributes. In compiling their lists of Americana in European representations, scholars have attached particular importance to feather-work and weapons – artefacts that could be found in European *Kunst- und Wunderkammern* – as a way of identifying otherwise unclassified human types as native Americans. Thus the club carried by the figure in Dürer's marginal sketch in the *Book of Hours* mentioned above is similar to a Tupinamba war club now in the Musée de l'Homme, Paris.[42]

Even if a human figure can be identified by virtue of one or more cultural attributes as a native American, this does not necessarily say anything about the context in which that figure appears. Just as the turkey could appear in the vicinity of scenes to which it had no relationship, or a South American macaw could feature as part of the natural setting of the island of Patmos – hardly an American venue – in a 1518 painting of St John by Burgkmair,[43] so figures endowed with American attributes could be included in scenes which had nothing to do with America. A painting attributed to Vasco Fernandes and dated to the first years of the sixteenth century has been taken to include a native Brazilian, identified as such on the basis of feathers and an arrow, in a scene which has no connection with America: the Adoration of the Magi.[44] Moreover, the message conveyed by the cultural attributes may not be unambiguous. The native Brazilian in this Portuguese *Adoration*, if that is what he is, nevertheless wears a European shirt and breeches. And though the coconut in his left hand could be American, the fact that it is mounted in silver is a clear indication that it is a European artefact.[45] Similarly, the attributes which have been identified as American in Dürer's marginal sketch, besides the club, are the Tupinamba feathered cloak, necklaces and bracelets of feathers with beads perhaps of wood, shell or bone 'typical of

Brazilian natives', and the cap, which has been called 'a real Tupinamba bonnet of small feathers fastened in the knots of a cotton net'.[46] However, the club has been lengthened into a lance and is carried in a way that betrays ignorance of its function; the feathered cloak is worn as a skirt; and the footwear is inappropriate (native Brazilians are said not to have worn sandals). And despite the presumed ethnographic accuracy of Weiditz's portraits of native Americans, who must have been Aztecs, one of them has a skirt-like row of feathers around his hips that is 'curiously similar to the Brazilian feather skirts',[47] suggesting contamination of Brazilian and Mexican attributes by the artist.[48] Such is the fluidity of such attributes that it is hazardous to assume that a human figure is a native American on the basis of a feathered skirt alone, since feathered skirts – an impractical item of clothing unlikely to have been worn by anybody in real life – appear in European representations not only of native Americans but also of Africans and Asians.[49] In compiling any corpus of images of America, there is thus a danger of maximizing it to include figures which are marked by a single presumed American attribute while discounting the presence of one or more non-American attributes in the same image. To label these figures as 'American' is misleading.

With these methodological provisos in mind, let us consider what has been called the earliest three-dimensional European representation of native Americans: the monument of Edmund Harman in the church of St John the Baptist, Burford, beside the River Windrush in Oxfordshire (illus. 68). Probably the best-known memorial stone in this church is the tablet given by the Workers' Educational Association in memory of three Levellers, Cornet Thompson, Corporal Perkins and John Church, shot on Oliver Cromwell's orders and buried in unmarked graves in the churchyard on 17 May 1649. Ever since the unveiling of the stone by Tony Benn in 1979, the church has become a *lieu de mémoire* of late twentieth-century British politics.

More fortunate than the three Levellers was Edmund Harman, one of the barbers of Henry VIII and a gentleman of his Privy Chamber, whose rise seems to have been associated with that of another Cromwell, Thomas, the 'hammer of the monks'. After the latter's execution in 1540, Harman was accused of heresy, but the King intervened, and all of the accused were pardoned. Apparently, Harman's influence was only enhanced by the experience, for in 1543 he and his wife Agnes received a grant of various lands in and around Burford. Agnes died in 1576; having remarried in the same year, Harman died in Burford a year later.[50]

68 Monument of Edmund Harman, 1569, St John the Baptist Church, Burford, Oxfordshire.

The north aisle of St John the Baptist contains a monument with a Latin inscription indicating that Harman erected it in 1569 'to the Christian memory of himself and his only and most faithful wife Agnes and of the sixteen children whom, by God's mercy, she bore him'. The lower half of the monument depicts the children in profile; the main panel is framed by a cartouche-like strap-work frame in which are four figures, naked except for what appear to be feathered head-dresses. On either side of them are long wooden sticks or clubs, to which a band of feathers and gourds are attached.

These four figures have been identified as Brazilian Tupinamba, the ethnic group most frequently associated with America in representations dating from the first half of the sixteenth century, and which exerted such a strong hold on the pictorial imagination that, in a process that has been called 'Tupinambization', they served as models for the depiction of North American Indians as well.[51] If this identification is correct, the Burford monument can be included in our list of *primeurs* as the earliest three-dimensional European representation of native Americans.

Twenty-five years ago, expert opinion on the subject was divided. Sturtevant expressed his doubts as to whether the Burford monument should be included in his checklist.[52] Stuart Piggott, on the other hand, accepted that the figures were New World Indians,[53] describing them as follows:

... strap-work within which, in place of the usual *putti* or *amorini*, four naked figures, recognisably those of American Indians with feather head-dresses, are symmetrically contrived, together with baskets of what may well be heads of maize, and unambiguous tropical fruit including gourds (*cucurbitae*). The sculpture is of a high quality and, in addition to the distinctive feather head-dresses, there has been a deliberate attempt to give the features a non-European appearance, even if they have in fact been rendered more Negroid than Amerindian in the process.[54]

It is a natural reflex to want to connect the iconography of a representation with the historical person with whom it is associated. In the case of a late eighteenth-century three-dimensional rendering of a native American, for example – one in John Flaxman's design for the memorial to Colonel John Graves Simcoe in Exeter Cathedral – the presence of such a figure on the funerary monument of a colonial official who had been involved in settling British–allied Indian groups within the provinces of Canada is easily explicable.[55] Or, to take a two-dimensional example, a portrait of Lady Elizabeth Pope, painted by Robert Peake to celebrate her marriage to Sir William Pope in 1615, displays a bracelet of pearls and coral, as well as a curious pattern of ostrich feathers on her mantle and hat. These details would seem to point towards exotic regions, and since Elizabeth was the only child of Sir Thomas Watson, one of the largest investors in the Virginia Company, these attributes might be taken to allude to America's riches, as well as tacitly suggesting an analogy between England's possession of the New World and Sir William's possession of his wife.[56] In the case of the Harman monument, one is therefore bound to ask whether there were any historical connections between Edmund Harman and the New World.

Piggott offers the following portrait of Edmund Harman:

Born c. 1509, a member of an Ipswich family, he became Barber Surgeon to Henry VIII, being admitted to the freedom of the Barber Surgeons' Company in 1530, and serving as Master in 1540; his portrait is included in the well-known painting by Holbein depicting the granting of the charter to the Company. In 1544 he was granted the Hospital of St John the Evangelist in Burford, and two years later the Manor of Taynton a couple of miles away; in the same year he was one of the witnesses to the will of Henry VIII, in which he was bequeathed £40. He married as his second wife a Burford woman, Agnes Sylvester, but at no time lived in that town, his country residence being in Taynton, where on his death in 1577, he expressed in his will his desire to be buried. He was in fact buried at Taynton but without a surviving monument.[57]

Nothing in this biographical sketch suggests a connection with America. Though Harman does appear to have had tenuous connections with foreign trade, there is nothing to substantiate any real link with the Americas. A possible connection that has been suggested lies in the fact that, as a member of the court, Harman must have seen the 'Brazilian king' who was taken to London and presented to Henry VIII by William Hawkins in 1532.[58] We have no way of knowing what impact, if any, this event had on Harman, nor are there grounds to see the four Brazilians on the Burford monument – if they are Brazilians at all – as *ad vivum* representations of that 'king'.

The late Michael Balfour drew on information concerning Harman that came to light after the publication of Piggott's article, but none of that material confirms any link with America either. He also mentioned the presentation to Henry VIII of the *Boke of Idrography* by the Dieppe cartographer Jean Rotz in 1542, a work that included maps of Brazil and a picture of a Tupinamban village that the author had visited in 1539.[59] But even if Harman knew about Rotz and his book, it is still a big leap from the *Boke of Idrography* to the Burford monument.

In short, if the figures on the Burford monument are to be interpreted as native Americans, there is as yet no substantiated link between Edmund Harman and the Americas. Thus the motivation for this iconographical motif remains unexplained.

But should the figures on the Burford monument be interpreted as Brazilians? Sturtevant was dismissive of Piggott's claims:

Piggott's identification rests primarily on the unclothed figures' strange headdresses, which vaguely resemble Brazilian feather crowns. They seem, however, to be similar to the Etruscan stylized palmettes which have been demonstrated to lie behind other 'headdresses' in sixteenth-century European depictions supposedly inspired by Aztec models. The other evidence Piggott cites is also shaky: the facial features are not so clearly non-European as they are stylized, and the odd ornaments do not seem 'unambiguous [representations of] tropical fruit including gourds.' Piggott was unable to adduce any American associations from the text of the monument or from what is known about the man who erected it.[60]

The Burford monument is thus not included in a list of Tupinamba-style representations published by Sturtevant in 1988.[61] At this point in the argument, the alleged iconographical link with America becomes as tenuous as the alleged connection of Edmund Harman with the New World.

The entire debate has overlooked the existence of a crucial 'third man' – the sculptor of the monument. The Lady Chapel of St John's contains a series of memorials to various members of the prosperous Sylvester family, extending from 1568 to 1904 (Harman's first wife was a Sylvester). The scrolled back-plate to the funerary monument of the first of the line, Edmund Sylvester, has a pattern derived from the Mannerist architect Sebastiano Serlio; the frieze on the Harman memorial has the same source. But the borrowing by the Harman monument sculptor went even further. The strap-work cartouche and the four exotic figures were in fact taken from a series of cartouches containing grotesque ornamental designs made by the Netherlandish artist Cornelis Bos (*c.* 1510–1555) around the middle of the sixteenth century. In the engraving reproduced here (illus. 69), the cartouche frames a landscape, while in another version it frames a French proverb, 'Vilain est qui faict les Villanies.' In neither case is there any obvious connection between the cartouche and what it frames.[62]

It has been suggested that one of the sources for Bos's grotesques was the Mexican objects on show in Brussels in 1520.[63] In that case, the model for the Burford monument would, through Bos's mediation, still be an American one. However, most of his grotesques date

69 Copper engraving after Cornelis Bos.

from a much later time, after his departure from Antwerp to Nürnberg in 1546. It is thus more likely that his work was influenced not by a display of Americana but by the work of his contemporaries in Paris and Germany (he may have spent part of 1544–5 in the French capital, where he would have come into contact with the School of Fontainebleau and the experiments of French book illustrators with strap-work and grotesques).[64]

The Burford sculptor deviated from his model on a few points. The arrangement of the tropical fruit is slightly different, and while the fruit on the left side of the cartouche appears to dangle from a cord (a loop is visible behind the forearm of the figure in the upper left), the fruit seems to be attached to what are presumably twisted wooden poles in the stone representation. Moreover, while a spray of leaves marks the point at which cord meets fruit in the cartouche, the leaves seem to have been replaced by feathers on the Harman monument.

In view of the fact that the poles on the monument are based on cords in the print, any resemblance between the combination of pole and feather decoration in the monument and Brazilian Tupinamba lances with their feather decoration (such as those in the woodcut of a family of Indian cannibals in Jan van Doesborch's *Of the newe landes* [1510–15]) can only be fortuitous. Thus one of the features which Piggott cited in support of his identification of the figures as Brazilian Indians is invalidated.

To turn to what Piggott refers to as feather head-dresses, they are less spiky than the crowns of upright, pointed feathers to be found on many of the Tupinamba representations, as well as on the Tupinamba feather crown now in the Ethnographic Museum in Copenhagen.[65] Perhaps the closest parallel is in the portrait of Quoniambec, the Tupinamba 'chief' illustrated in all of André Thevet's published works on America.[66] The muscular physique and protruding chin of the figures in the strap-work cartouche are also to be seen in the portrait of Quoniambec (see illus. 75).

To sum up so far: both the feathered head-dresses and the poles or lances with fruit on the Burford monument have parallels in sixteenth-century images of native America, although the parallelism of the poles turns out to be chimerical. However, the remaining attributes – tropical produce in the form of maize and baskets of fruit – also appear on a woodcut made by Hans Burgkmair around 1517 for *The Triumph of Maximilian*, in which some of 'the people of Calicut' have attributes which Sturtevant and others have identified as native American.[67]

But the existence of parallels with images of native America does not mean that the figures on the monument should necessarily be identified as native Americans. In other words, we can only proceed from establishing the *parallel* to making the *identification* if we can be sure that there are no other candidates.

This is where Sturtevant's reference to Etruscan palmettes becomes crucial.[68] He is in fact referring to an important article by the Belgian art historian Nicole Dacos, in which she argues that the source of the feather or metal strip arrangements frequently used by Bos lies in the leaf decorations of antique Italian, particularly Etruscan, art, and that a revival of these themes in the early sixteenth century had more to do with the discovery around 1480 of the decorations in the Domus Aurea in Rome than with the influence of Americana.[69]

Dacos' argument has enormous implications for those who set out to establish a corpus of images of America, because it calls into question the automatic way in which crowns consisting of upright feathers or metal strips have been taken to be evocations of that continent. If we view the alleged native American in the early Portuguese *Adoration of the Magi* in light of these considerations, the upright 'feathers' of his crown (they actually look quite metallic) can be seen to resemble the splayed diadem revealed by X-rays in Giorgione's famous painting in Vienna traditionally known as *The Three Philosophers* – a painting that dates from the same years as the Portuguese picture.[70] In the face of these parallels, it becomes increasingly difficult to maintain a native American identification of the figure in the Portuguese *Adoration*.

Now that we have managed to draw the figures in the Burford monument and in the cartouche on which it depends away from a direct dependence on Americana, it is logical to compare them with other works within their genre: grotesque ornamentation. The evidence is overwhelming: a glance through any catalogue of French, Netherlandish or Italian grotesques from the second half of the sixteenth century is enough to show that neither the gourds attached to poles nor the feathered (or metallic) head-dresses are unique to the monument or the cartouche.[71]

If we recall the lessons drawn from the analysis of natural-historical representations of native America in the sixteenth century – one of which, the ornamental cartouche after Léonard Thiry (see illus. 59), belongs to the same genre of grotesques – we see that they also hold in the case of the Bos cartouche and the Burford monument. Here, too, it proves very difficult to draw a line between fact and fantasy. Are these figures supposed to be native Americans, or are they to be classified among the fantastic creatures that populate many ornamental prints? And even if it is possible (though not necessary) to identify the human figures as native Americans by virtue of one or more of their cultural attributes, this does not necessarily make the context in which these figures appear an American one.

As a result of this analysis, the lives of the images on the Burford monument have undergone a metamorphosis. Behind an iconography that has parallels in European representations of native Americans, we discover a longer history going back to the art of ancient Italy and Etruria, and resurfacing not in the discovery of the New World but in the re-discovery of the Old World with the excavation of Nero's Domus Aurea in the Renaissance. Moreover, this history was mediated through the work of an artist from the Netherlands who probably encountered it on his involuntary travels through France and Germany.

Where does this leave the category of 'first images'? I have argued above that classification of the grotesques in the Bos cartouche and their three-dimensional counterparts on the Burford monument is consonant with sixteenth-century images of native Americans. By the criteria of twentieth-century iconographical analysis and interpretation, they could thus be identified as American. But this does not mean that they were seen as such in the sixteenth century. Given the other contexts which they could evoke (the fantastic, mythological world of the grotesque ornament, as well as the world of Roman and Etruscan antiquity), it seems rather narrow-minded to want to pin them down to an exclusively American context.

If the category 'first images of America' seems too narrow, I would suggest that images of this kind be classified as typical of what can be called the 'exotic genre'. Within representations of this type, elements or attributes from different geographical locations could be juxtaposed without necessarily connoting any specific geographical point of reference. What was important was not their geographical provenance but their exoticism.

This view finds support if we briefly consider another early representation that has been taken by some scholars to be the first painting of native Americans: the panel now known as *West Indian Landscape* by the Netherlandish painter Jan Mostaert, probably dating from the 1520s or '30s (illus. 70). The scene is that of the incursion of European invaders into an idyllic landscape recalling renderings of primitive civilization by the Italian painter Piero di Cosimo.[72] As I have argued elsewhere, the presence of white-trimmed red Tartar caps, classical trumpets, fauns with pointed ears, Netherlandish costume and European fauna (sheep, cows, a hare, a hedgehog and rabbits)

70 Jan Mostaert, *West Indian Landscape*, second quarter of the 16th century, oil on panel.

does not rule out the possibility that Mostaert's picture may refer to what he imagined a New World landscape might look like.[73] The application of the label 'West Indian' or 'American' probably assumes a greater degree of specificity than the limits of the exotic genre allow, however.

If we include the Burford monument in the exotic genre, there is no need to assume that the figures in the frame, even if they resemble European representations of Brazilian Tupinamba, were taken to be specifically American by the sculptor. As elements of the grotesque, they no more connoted America than fauns, satyrs and so on necessarily connoted Greco-Roman antiquity. More generally, an important methodological lesson can be drawn in connection with the attempt to define any corpus of representations of America: that sixteenth-century iconography did not always operate along the same lines as those followed by its more recent practitioners. And as the practice of iconographical analysis itself changes over time, the boundaries of any corpus of representations of America will be bound to change too. To repeat: the limits of such a corpus are undecidable.

This absolves us of the need to look for a connection between Edmund Harman and America. As we have seen, nothing in the life of this English barber-surgeon suggests any special connection with that continent.

Finally, it should be noted that a crude copy of the Bos cartouche was used for the Thomas Tipping monument erected in 1595 in the church of Ickford in Buckinghamshire, about 25 miles from Burford. The same engraving was used in the gallery of Wolfeton House, Charminster, Dorset, which was rebuilt around 1600. Other Bos plates were used in houses near Bristol and in Sussex.[74] Thus our examination of the Harman monument tells us less about early images of America than it does about the influence of Continental designs on art and decoration in Elizabethan and Jacobean England.

4 The Purloined Codex

Mexican pictorial screen-folds or codices often travelled as widely as the images we have been considering. For example, a codex describing the origins of the Mixtec lords and genealogical history of Tilantongo was in Europe by 1521, passing via Portugal to Rome, where a young Medici cardinal inherited it from Pope Clement VII. After the cardinal's death, the book was taken to Germany, where it was later purchased by Duke Albrecht V of Bavaria for his collection. During the German wars with Sweden, it came into the possession of the Duke of Sachsen-Weimar, whose descendant presented it to the Emperor of Austria. Summing up this history, Mixtec expert Maarten Jansen wrote: 'Thus, the document became the "Codex Vienna", or in Latin, "Vindobonensis", totally divorced from its ancient Mixtec context and, therefore, quite incomprehensible to its new owners.'[1] Images from it already began to circulate in the seventeenth century, when the German philologist Hiob Ludolf, who had copied part of folio 12r when he saw the codex in Weimar, gave his drawing to the famous Danish collector Olaus Worm during a visit to Copenhagen. Worm included it in the publication about his collection entitled *Museum Wormianum*, referring to it as a 'Mexican hieroglyphic'.[2]

Many of those through whose hands these codices passed had no inkling of what the images contained within them were meant to represent. The codices functioned as curiosities, and it is usually descriptions of their physical appearance that turn up in collection inventories, where they often appear alongside antiquities. The extent to which their presence in collections may be said to have helped spread knowledge about indigenous American writing systems thus remains questionable.[3] It is appropriate here to follow the dictum of the detective hero, C. Auguste Dupin, in Edgar Allan Poe's *The Purloined Letter*, that 'If it is any point requiring reflection, we shall examine it to better purpose in the dark.' The material examined in the present chapter will be considered in this way, largely without taking its meaning for and within native American cultures into account. Instead, we shall follow the disappearance of certain motifs, their subterranean survival and their re-emergence in different places and at different times.

As we saw in Chapter 1, one of the classic discussions of the migration of images is Wittkower's 'Eagle and Serpent' article, which deals *inter alia* with the motif of the eagle tearing a serpent whilst sitting on a nopal cactus.[4] This image, which is still used by the Mexican Republic as a coat-of-arms and on coins, was also the glyph for Tenochtitlán, the centre of Aztec civilization, founded in the year Two House (AD 1325) and commemorated on the first page of the *Codex Mendoza* (illus. 71). Let us begin, then, with this codex.

The *Codex Mendoza*, now in the Bodleian Library, Oxford, is a 71-folio work consisting of three parts. The first is a chronicle of Aztec rulers; the second is a tribute list, organized by region; the third deals with the life and customs of the Mexica-Aztec. The association of this work with the name Mendoza is not without its problems. In 1780, the Jesuit Francisco Javier Clavigero (1721–1787), author of a famous apology for Aztec culture, *Storia antica del Messico*, was the first to associate the codex with Antonio de Mendoza, who served the Spanish Crown as Viceroy of New Spain from 1535 to 1550. Mendoza was reported to be preparing a 'relation of the things of this land' in 1541, and it must have been at about the same time that the Viceroy inspected a pictorial manuscript in Mexico City in the house of a native *maestro de los pintores*. However, there are some difficulties in assuming that the codex now in Oxford is to be identified with the work commissioned by Mendoza, for the latter seems to have included the years of the conquest, which are absent from the *Codex Mendoza*.

It is with more certainty that we can establish the connection between the *Codex Mendoza* and the Franciscan friar André Thevet.[5] Thevet served as chaplain to the Frenchman Villegagnon on the latter's expedition to Brazil in 1555, but he was taken ill and returned to France only ten weeks after his arrival. The 1557 publication of Thevet's *Les Singularitez de la France Antarctique*, in which ethnographic motifs from the area of Rio de Janeiro are associated with parallel customs from antiquity, permitted the inhabitants of the New World to be seen as a part of 'history'. Thevet's work was rapidly translated into Italian and English,[6] and the man himself rose to obtain a number of important clerical and courtly positions, including that of royal cosmographer to four successive French kings.

The fact that the *Codex Mendoza* bears five ex libris bearing

71 The founding of Tenochtitlán, capital of the Aztec Empire, in the year Two House (AD 1325), from *Codex Mendoza*, second quarter of the 16th century, pigment on European paper.

Thevet's name, two of them including the date 1553, is a clear enough indication that it passed through his hands.[7] According to his own account, a French corsair purloined the codex on its way to Spain. The corsair gave it to the French King, who in turn passed it on to Thevet. A note on the manuscript's cover indicates that Thevet had sold it to the English geographer and historian Richard Hakluyt by 1587 at the latest. On Hakluyt's death in 1616, it passed into the hands of Samuel Purchas, who continued Hakluyt's work of collecting and publishing material on travels. Purchas's son acquired it later, and from him it ended up in the collection of John Selden, finding its way into the Bodleian in 1659.

So much for the transmission history of the artefact itself. Publication of the codex can be said to have begun with that of a number of woodcuts based on it in Volume III of Purchas's *Hakluytus Posthumus, or Purchas, His Pilgrimes* (illus. 72), although there were numerous errors in transcription and translation, and the woodcuts Purchas used were considered by one authority to be so crude as to be 'mere bibliographical curiosities' today.[8] Nevertheless, these woodcuts were

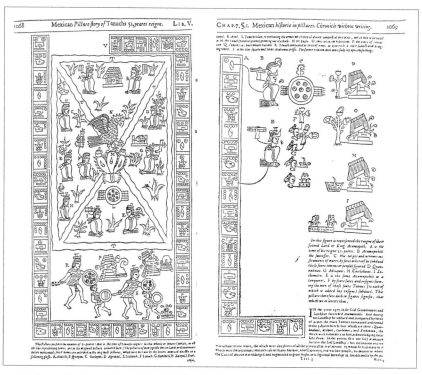

72 Woodcuts taken from fols 2r and 2v of *Codex Mendoza*, in Samuel Purchas, *Hakluytus Posthumus, or Purchas, His Pilgrimes* (London, 1625).

used for the second (1630) edition of De Laet's *History of the New World*; Athanasius Kircher copied them in his vast study of hieroglyphic writing, *Oedipus Aegyptiacus*; they were used in Melchisedec Thévenot's *Histoire de l'empire mexicain* (illus. 73); and Warburton drew on them in *The Divine Legation of Moses Demonstrated* (1738–41).[9]

That Thevet's interest in the civilization of Central America extended to the use of original sources can be seen if we consider the case of his *Histoyre du Méchique*, an 88-folio manuscript fragment which was probably intended to be inserted in his *Cosmographie universelle* (1575). The first part of this manuscript is a faithful translation of parts of Gonzalo Fernández de Oviedo's *Historia general y natural de las Indias*; the second part is a unique document assumed to go back either to a lost work by the Franciscan scholar Andrés de Olmos or to another Spanish original, perhaps accompanied by pictographic elements.[10]

In light of his interest in these sources, and given the fact that the *Codex Mendoza* was in his possession for some 30 years, there is good reason to suppose that Thevet might also have drawn on it as a source. It was not necessary for him to be able to understand the pictorial language, because each section of the codex was accompanied by a Spanish text or gloss based on interpretation of the signs by knowledgeable Indian elders. Indeed, it has been demonstrated that a number of the features of Thevet's survey of Aztec civilization in the *Cosmographie universelle* were taken from the *Codex Mendoza*.[11]

Another work of Thevet's is highly relevant in this connection: his *Les Vrais Pourtraits et Vies des Hommes Illustres Grecz, Latins, et Payens Recuilliz de Leurs Tableaux Livres, Medalles antiques, et Modernes*, a collection of portraits and lives of dead popes, bishops, warriors, poets and others, published in Paris in 1584.[12] The immediate precedent for this work was the Italian Humanist Paolo Giovio's collection of portraits of famous men, of which a French translation had appeared as *Les Eloges et Vies briefvement descrites sous les images des plus illustres et principaux hommes de guerre, antiques et modernes*, in 1559. Giovio included African and Asian kings among his portraits, and Thevet followed suit by including a number of exotic sitters, though in his case they extended to the New World.[13] Book VIII, dedicated to 'emperors and kings', contains portraits of the following celebrities: Julius Caesar; 'Ferguz first king of Scotland'; Saladin, Sultan of Egypt; Tamerlane, Emperor of the Tartars; Mahomet II; Tomombey, last sultan of Egypt; 'Atabalipa, Roy du Péru'; 'Motzume, Roy de Mexique'; 'Cherif, roy de Fez et de Marroc';

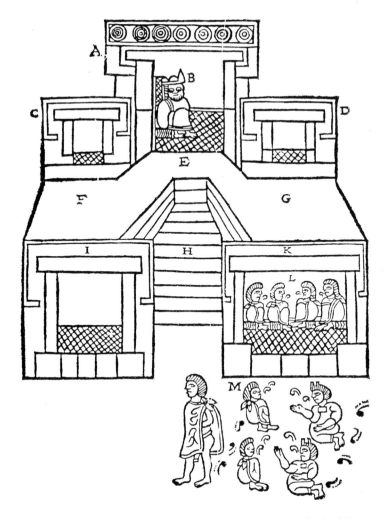

73 Title page image to Melchisedec Thévenot, *Histoire de l'empire mexicain* (Paris, 1696), showing Motecuhzoma ('with Beard') in his palace, taken from Purchas's woodcut of a folio from *Codex Mendoza*.

'Barberousse, admiral pour le Turc en la mer du Levant'; 'Nacol-Absou, Roy du promontoire des Cannibales'; Sultan Mustapha, the son of Sultan Soliman; 'Paracoussi, Roy de Platte'; 'Hismael Sophi, Roy de Perse'; 'Quoniambec' and 'Paraousti Satouriona, Roy de la Floride'.[14]

Writing in 1976, Sturtevant did not find Thevet's portraits of Atahualpa and Motecuhzoma very convincing; his verdict fifteen years later was still that they were 'quite dubious'.[15] It was the German art historian Rüdiger Joppien who first suggested in 1978 that some of them might have derived from an ethnographically reliable source, which he identified as the *Codex Mendoza*.[16] The immediate pictorial sources for the 'cannibal king' Nacol-Absou (illus. 74) and the Brazilian 'chief' Quoniambec (illus. 75) can easily be dispensed with, for they derived from the woodcuts in Thevet's own *Cosmographie universelle*; that of Paracoussi (illus. 76) will be discussed later. The test case for Joppien's argument is the portrait of Motecuhzoma (illus. 77). Joppien drew attention to the feather-work shield which the ruler is carrying; this is known from several Aztec manuscripts as a mark of rank. The presence of one stylized half-moon in the shield's upper segment and of three half-moons in the lower segment enabled Joppien to identify it as Huaztec. Joppien went on to claim that Motecuhzoma 's clothing should be regarded as another indication that the artist intended to depict items of Mexican origin. Thus his tunic, with a knot tied over the left shoulder, is closely paralleled in the figure of a warrior depicted in the *Codex Mendoza* (illus. 78). The shield carried by this warrior is very similar to that carried by Motecuhzoma; the differences lie in the arrangement of the horizontal bands and that of the decorative feather-work border beneath the shield, as well as the encrustations of three shells on the upper horizontal band. Motecuhzoma's diadem, with a triangular point in front and a turquoise inset, is found in several illustrations in the *Codex Mendoza*, though the feathers are an addition by the European artist.[17]

Joppien did not mention that the *Codex Mendoza* actually contains *two* representations of Motecuhzoma. The first of these occurs in the chronicle of Aztec rulers with which the codex begins (illus. 79). Motecuhzoma Xocoyotzin ('the younger') (1502–1520), ninth in the series, is depicted seated on a woven mat and wrapped in a plain white cloak that covers him from neck to ankle. He wears a turquoise headband with a red back-tie. Above his head is his name glyph: a headband resting on a hairpiece or wig along with turquoise nose and ear ornaments. There is no glyph for the second part of his name ('younger').

If this figure is compared with the portrait by Thevet's artist,[18] we can note a number of differences. The pose has been changed from a seated to a standing one. The cloak has been replaced by a tunic, leaving the arms bare. The shield and lance, as Joppien indicated, were not taken from the portrait of Motecuhzoma but from the iconography of the Mexica warrior. The shield depicted, of the so-called *cuexyo* type, occurs in the *Codex Mendoza*. In fact, it is the commonest type depicted there.[19]

In compiling what is thus a composite portrait of Motecuhzoma

74 'Nacol-Absou, Roy du promontoire des Cannibales', engraving from André Thevet, *Les Vrais Pourtraits et Vies des Hommes Illustres …* (Paris, 1584).

75 'Quoniambec', engraving from Thevet, *Les Vrais Pourtraits …*

76 'Paracoussi, Roy de Platte', engraving, from Thevet, *Les Vrais Pourtraits* …

77 'Motzume, Roy de Mexique', engraving, from Thevet, *Les Vrais Pourtraits* …

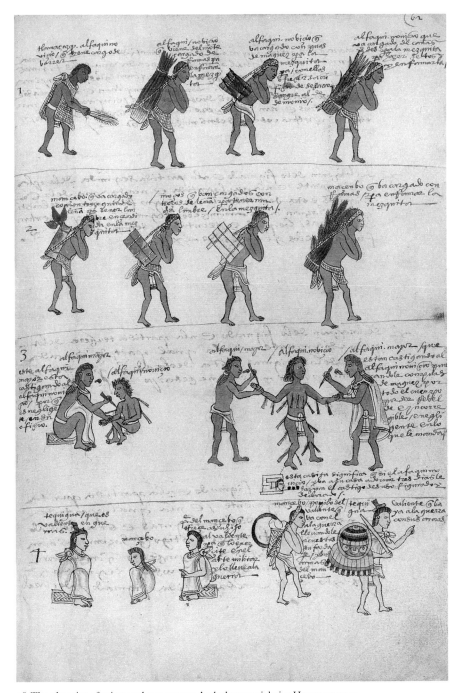

78 The education of priests and commoners. At the bottom right is a Huaxtec *cuexyo* shield decorated with crescent-shaped nose ornaments. From *Codex Mendoza*.

79 Motecuhzoma (without beard) and his conquests, from *Codex Mendoza*.

from different sections of the *Codex Mendoza*, the artist ignored the second portrait of Motecuhzoma the Younger, which is found in the section dealing with the life and customs of the Mexica on which Thévenot drew for the title page to his *Histoire de l'empire mexicain* (see illus. 73). That there are stylistic variations between the codex's different sections is immediately apparent in this portrait of Motecuhzoma. Wearing a plain turquoise cloak (*tilmatli*), he is portrayed within a palace. The use of the *en-face* convention, the attempt at perspective in the rendering of the palace,[20] and the use of shading to indicate depth are evidence that we are dealing with the product of an artist who was influenced by European artistic conventions. Most strikingly, this Motecuhzoma is bearded.

We may therefore conclude by noting that the portrait is a work of both combination and selection, in which certain iconographic elements contained in the *Codex Mendoza*, though not those which had undergone European influence, were combined to produce a portrait that could nevertheless hold its own within a series of depictions of illustrious men.

However, the parallels which Joppien adduced from the *Codex Mendoza* in connection with the portrait of Atahualpa (illus. 80) are less convincing. In the portrait by Thevet's artist, this ruler wears a diadem surmounted by feathers and a bundle of feathers attached to the rear of the crown and falling behind his shoulders. He wears a garment folded over the right shoulder which covers the upper arms but leaves the forearms exposed. This garment has a decorated border of alternating black and white squares. All of these details can be matched in the *Codex Mendoza*, but there are differences too. The authentic feather-work of Atahualpa's crown is combined with inlaid stones which are closer to European conventions, like the diadem with triangular points and inset stones worn by Fergus, King of Scotland. Though Atahualpa's garment, including the decorative border, has parallels in the codex (which it resembles much more closely than the Peruvian decorations later depicted by Guaman Poma de Ayala), the treatment of the sleeves does not; in fact, it has its closest parallel in the tunic worn by Julius Caesar, which is fastened in a knot over the right shoulder and has the sleeves drawn back to reveal the forearms. The most striking adaptation of the codex, however, is the pectoral with rosettes. As Joppien pointed out,[21] the circular decorative motif on the coloured tunics of the Aztec warriors is the precedent for Atahualpa's pectoral, but the latter has been reduced to the size of a medallion; and whereas the motifs in the codex are part of the decoration of the fabric itself, the pectoral depicted by Thevet's artist,

'Atabalipa, Roy du Pérou', engraving from Thevet, *Les Vrais Pourtraits* …

through its close proximity to the chain that dangles from Atahualpa's neck (the bound figure of Atahualpa has its parallel in that of Tomombey, whose arms are bound with ropes), seems to be hanging from it rather than attached to his garment.[22]

Finally, let us consider the portrait of 'Paraousti Satouriona, Roy de la Floride' by Thevet's artist (illus. 81). This figure, dressed in an animal skin, wears a helmet made from what is apparently a lynx (to judge from the tufted ears). Joppien here adduced a parallel with the depiction of a priest-warrior from the *Codex Mendoza* (illus. 82). This figure is carrying a *cuexyo* shield (like Thevet's Motecuhzoma) and has a long hair-piece of feathers attached to the rear of his head (like

81 'Paraousti Satouriona, Roy de la Floride', engraving from Thevet, *Les Vrais Pourtraits* …

Thevet's Atahualpa). Moreover, his body is encased in an animal skin, while his head is encased in an animal head as a helmet, which Joppien took to be like Thevet's King of Florida.

However, there are striking differences. While the animal head in the codex covers almost the entire head of the warrior, who has to peer through an opening between its jaws, the helmet of Paraousti Satouriona is cut away beneath the feline's nose, leaving his face unprotected. The animal's teeth, so conspicuous in the codex, are absent in the Thevetian portrait. Moreover, while the animal skin fits the warrior in the codex like a diving suit, the Floridian's outfit is kept in place by a knot consisting of the feline's paws on his chest, like the

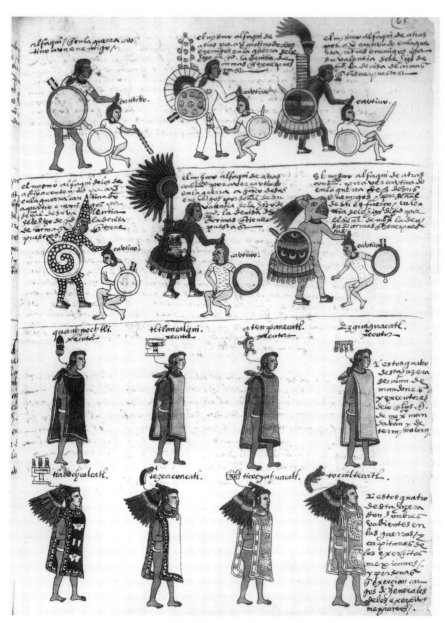

82 The six ranks of the priest-warrior. The image on the far right of register 2 is the six-captive priest-warrior wearing the yellow coyote costume. From *Codex Mendoza*.

hooves of the animal skin knotted around the figure of Paracoussi.

In fact, the closest parallel to the King of Florida is to be found not in the folios of the *Codex Mendoza* but in Greco-Roman portrayals of the hero Herakles/Hercules, who regularly wears a lion skin knotted in this way. This is precisely how Thevet himself described the Indians of eastern Canada, where the men wore their hair 'like a horse's tail, with wooden needles through it', and, on top of that, 'a skin of a tiger, bear or other beast'. In fact, their costume reminded him of the theatre, 'looking most like the portraits of Hercules which the ancient Romans made for their amusement'.[23] Thevet's visual and textual portrayals of Quoniambec, the Brazilian 'chief' (see illus. 75), also have a Herculean colouring.[24]

Besides this model from classical antiquity, there was another one available to Thevet's artist: the iconography of the early Germanic peoples. The works of the philologist Justus Lipsius and others from the last decades of the sixteenth century reveal the existence of a 'Batavian' iconography in which members of the German nobility were depicted dressed in animal skins and using the heads of animals as helmets (illus. 83).[25] As happened so often, a conflation took place between Europe's 'primitive' others from the past and its 'exotic' others from the present.

It is worth considering a few of the factors that appear to have governed the hand and eye of Thevet's artist. The first of these is what can be called an 'aristocratic filter'. As we have seen, there was an immediate precedent for Thevet's collection of engravings in those based on the portraits in the collection of Paolo Giovio (who was said to have given Vasari the idea of writing his *Lives of the Artists*). The ancient precedent for cycles of *uomini famosi* was Varro's *Hebdomades*, which, the elder Pliny tells us, consisted of seven hundred biographies accompanied by effigies based on statues or coins.[26] Cycles of this kind became popular in Italy from the end of the fourteenth century; a well-known example from around 1480 is the series of famous secular and religious figures illustrating the major intellectual disciplines of the time in the *studiolo* of Federico da Montefeltro in Urbino.[27] In France, Thevet had apparently been planning something along the lines of *Les Vrais Pourtraits et Vies* since the middle of the century, but the publication in 1553 of the *Promptuaire des médailles* by Guillaume Rouillé, with portraits of famous personages from Adam and Eve down to the French monarch Henri II, took the wind out of Thevet's sails. However, his decision to postpone publication enabled him to collect additional portraits, drawing among others on the assemblage owned by Catherine de' Medici.[28] Together, the

83 Warriors in animal skins armed with clubs, engraving from Philipp Clüver, *De Germania Antiqua* (Leiden, 1616).

Lib. 1, Pag. 300. figura II.

portrait galleries in the courtly *Kunstkammern* of Europe and their reproductions in collections of engravings provided an aristocratic setting which left its mark on Thevet's 'ethnographic' portraits. For instance, the interest in Motecuhzoma's feather-work shield and the device on Paracoussi's shield betray not only ethnographic curiosity but also a desire to render a theme dear to European nobility: heraldry. This perspective is particularly evident in Thevet's treatment of the Brazilian 'chief' Quoniambec (see illus. 75), who combines physical criteria of excellence – an athletic frame and bulging muscles – with a remarkable adaptation of the ethnographic panoply of Brazil to the accoutrements of a European-style monarch. Thus the feather diadem was interpreted as a crown, and – whatever its original function may have been – his staff became a royal sceptre in Thevet's interpretation.[29]

This process of iconographic assimilation of native Americans to European royalty was in conformity with the actual practice of Europeans towards those they regarded as their American counterparts. Cortés's gifts to Motecuhzoma of an armchair and a crimson cap have their parallel in the European practice of dressing other principals in one's own princely accoutrements, and both the theory and practice of religious reverence in New Spain assumed a functional equivalence between the Indian upper classes and their Spanish counterparts.[30] At the same time, this was part of a broader process of assimilation in which things American were viewed through European eyes, of which the aristocratic filter constituted one particular refraction. We have seen this process at work in the hands of Thevet's artist in the treatment of the physique of his subjects, the European sleeves of Atahualpa, or the Herculean iconography of the King of Florida; many other examples could be added from the earliest sixteenth-century images of America.

On the other hand, we have noted how Thevet's artist preferred the more 'exotic' rendering of Motecuhzoma in the *Codex Mendoza* to the more European portrait of the same person later in the same codex. The reason for this choice probably lay in what we might call a penchant for the exotic: it was the more exotic, and therefore the more striking, version of Motecuhzoma which, precisely because it was exotic, conferred greater interest on it as a subject. In an era when singularity attracted attention – we might recall that Thevet's first publication on the Americas was entitled *Les Singularitez de la France Antarctique* – there was a premium on the (relatively) brilliant and bizarre above the (relatively) commonplace.

As a corollary, specific geographical provenance was of less importance than the capacity of the singularity to partake in a world of exotica in general. This indifference to geographical detail is evident in the choice of models from the *Codex Mendoza* for both Motecuhzoma and Atahualpa, despite the fact that Peru was not Mexico. Indeed, Thevet's reference to the plumage attached to Paracoussi's head as coming from the Hyona bird, a name which he claimed was Persian (!) for pigeon, betrays a bewildering approach to geographical specificity. But this is not the only confusion: in view of the inconsistencies between Thevet's text and the illustration of 'Paracoussi, Roy de Platte' (which Thevet claimed was made after a portrait from life by a sailor who had visited Río de la Plata), it has been suggested that Thevet transposed the captions of his portraits of Paracoussi and of the Floridan king Paraousti Satouriona. In particular, while Thevet's text on Paracoussi mentions that his nose was pierced with a stone, this feature is to be found not in the visual portrait of Paracoussi (see illus. 76) but in that of Paraousti Satouriona (see illus. 81).[31] Despite attempts to revise Thevet's bad reputation as an ethnographer, we are bound to admit that, like most of his contemporaries, he tended to view America as a relatively homogeneous entity. In the case of Peru, although some printed reports had been published by this time, it is doubtful whether Thevet had a very clear idea about its boundaries – or of those of Brazil or Mexico, for that matter.[32] A similar confusion, or lack of specificity, can be observed in Montaigne's essay *Des Coches*, in which the states of Mexico and Peru are both viewed through Brazilian eyes.[33] F. Lestringant's characterization of Montaigne's geography as 'aleatory' is just as true of Thevet's geographical conceptions.[34]

The American portraits in Thevet's *Les Vrais Pourtraits et Vies* can thus be shown to display four main characteristics: an aristocratic filter, a penchant for the exotic, a tendency towards European assimilation, and a vagueness with regard to geography. These four characteristics can also be found in sixteenth-century European collections of curiosities.[35] For instance, the aristocratic filter is displayed in the focus on musical instruments and weapons in Montaigne's collection of curiosities. The penchant for the exotic is evident from the lists of objects included in such collections, such as eagle stones, coral, fossils, petrified objects, mandrake roots, barnacle geese, birds of paradise, flying fish, mermaids, chameleons, toucans, the bones of giants, canoes, armadillos, weapons, Egyptian mummies, unicorns' horns, feathered head-dresses and musical instruments. The tendency towards European assimilation is particularly evident in labelling attached to genuine or assumed religious articles, such as the Inuit woman's sealskin parka given to Marchese Ferdinando Cospi by the painter Michelango Colonna, which entered a Baroque theatre of marvels when Cospi's collection was annexed to that of the Bolognese polymath Ulisse Aldrovandi in 1657. Illustrated in the inventory of the Museo Cospiano compiled a decade later, the parka was labelled as 'a garment of an Indian priest'. Indifference towards geographic provenance can be seen in the wide range of meanings covered by the epithet 'Indian', the assumption that the characters on Mexican codices were Chinese, the labelling of a kayak as 'a leathern Japanese little ship' and so on.[36]

We can therefore put forward two contexts against which Thevet's ethnographic portraits should be set: not just the series of illustrious men who adorned the walls of many a *Kunstkammer*, but the collections of novelties and curiosities that filled the Renaissance

Wunderkammern. We should be wary of setting up a rigid division between these two contexts, for though it may be analytically useful to distinguish between them, the collecting activities of Paolo Giovio referred to earlier are a good instance of how these two contexts could be combined: besides the portraits of *uomini famosi*, Giovio's collection also included exotic objects from Asia and America, many of them derived from the spoils of the Turkish corsair and scourge of the eastern Mediterranean, Barbarossa Khayr ad-Din.[37] The collection of Archduke Ferdinand II at Schloß Ambras displayed a similar combination of busts of illustrious historical figures (in the *Antiquarium*) with natural and artificial curiosities (in the *Kunstkammer*).[38]

Behind this practice of collecting, we may tentatively identify a way of looking at the world. As Carlo Ginzburg demonstrated in an essay on Montaigne, the way in which the latter approached the New World was in the spirit of just such collections of curiosities: '... in his essay on cannibals Montaigne unfolded what we may call the moral and intellectual implications of the Wunderkammer.'[39] Both Montaigne and Thevet were collectors: they regarded the New World as a source of collectibles, and this aesthetic governed the way they portrayed, in text or in image, New World peoples. The *Codex Mendoza* itself, and the portraits based on it, were both items that could be collected, and indeed they were, by Thevet.

Sturtevant compared Thevet's portrait of Atahualpa to the portrait of 'Athabalippa Rex ultimus Americae' (illus. 84) issued three years earlier by Abraham de Bruijn in his *Omnium pene Europeae, Asiae, Aphricae atque Americae gentium habitus*, and other Thevet woodcuts bear comparison with other American figures in the same compilation;[40] the latter in turn should be compared with figures in the earlier costume books by Nicolas de Nicolay, François Desprès and Johannes Sluperius.[41] Interest in portraying national costumes goes back at least to the end of the fifteenth century, when Dürer depicted Venetian and Ottoman costumes during his first Italian journey. The earliest of the collections of depictions of national costumes is apparently Christoph Weiditz's *Trachtenbuch*, a collection of 154 folios containing ink or watercolour portraits of national types produced between 1529 and 1532, but the genre did not really get under way until the publication of François Desprès' *Recueil de la diversité des habits* by Richard Breton in Paris in 1562. It reached its apogee at the end of the century with Cesare Vecellio's *Habiti antichi e moderni di tutto il mondo* (1598). The exact place of Thevet's *Les Vrais Pourtraits et Vies* within this body of material has yet to be determined.[42]

Nobilis femina in America.   Athabalippa Rex vltimus Americæ

84 'Nobilis femina in America' and 'Athabalippa Rex ultimus Americae', engraving from
Abraham de Bruijn, *Omnium pene Europae, Asiae, Aphricae atque Americae gentium habitus*
(Antwerp, 1581).

In considering the period after Thevet, one could write two histories. One would be that of the influence of Thevet's work (both texts
and images) on the steadily growing body of literature on America.
For example, his images deriving from the *Codex Mendoza* appear to
have had an immediate impact on the French artist Jacques Le Moyne
de Morgues. Le Moyne, who had accompanied René de Laudonnière
on the disastrous French expedition to Florida in 1564, was commissioned by Theodor de Bry, publisher of various accounts of travel to
the New World, to provide the illustrations for Volume 11 of the
Great Voyages, published in 1591. As Le Moyne's originals have not
survived, any assessment of them has to rely on the engravings that
were finally published in De Bry's compilation, but the question of
the extent to which these should be regarded as De Bry's rather than
Le Moyne's work does not alter the fact that they betray a dependence on Thevet.[43]

    As for the subsequent influence and reception of Thevet, there is
no need to repeat what Lestringant has written on the period from
1592, culminating in Flaubert's *Tentation de saint Antoine*.[44] Both

Thevet's texts and his illustrations were widely used by other writers on natural history such as Ambroise Paré and Ulisse Aldrovandi, and his work acquired a particular status as a sourcebook on the fauna of the Americas.

The second history that could be written is that of the subsequent appreciation of the *Codex Mendoza*, ranging from Carlos de Sigüenza y Góngora's praise of Samuel Purchas for having published it to Cornelis de Pauw's negative verdict on the clumsy, crude drawings and lack of perspective; on the historical side, de Pauw suggested that the alleged list of eight kings who had preceded Motecuhzoma might be a list of that ruler's mistresses.[45]

The third history is one that is more difficult to write. The portraits by Thevet's artist had a life of their own, detached from their context either in the *Codex Mendoza* or in *Les Vrais Pourtraits et Vies*. There is some irony in the fact that, detached from the latter paper hall of fame, these images came to function in very different ways, this phenomenon too being characteristic of the Renaissance collection of curiosities. *Wunderkammern* contained objects from different contexts, recontextualizing them in new settings. For example, a famous greenstone mask in the collection of the Medici was set with rubies and mounted in a gilded copper frame to produce an exhibit severed from its original purpose, function or value.[46]

Tracking down cases of this kind is no easy business, for the simple reason that there is no *a priori* place to look for them. The first of these re-emergences turns up in what seems at first glance to be a surprising place: the parallel lives of great characters from Greek and Roman antiquity by Plutarch. The first edition of the translation of *The Lives of the Noble Grecians & Romans* made by Sir Thomas North, on which Shakespeare was to draw for his historical dramas (based on Jacques Amyot's translation of Plutarch into French), dates from 1579. The enlarged edition published in London in 1657, however, contains twenty engravings taken from Thevet, though reduced in size, in a prosopographical appendix. These include a number of exotic figures who had no connection with either Greece or Rome, including one American: 'Atabalipa, King of Peru', based on Thevet's engraving. Quoniambec was added to a new edition of the work ten years later.[47]

The relevance of American 'kings' for Plutarch's lives lies in the importance of the aristocratic filter. As Lestringant put it: 'Through a double process of heroization and moralization, one sees "the most cruel of the universe" allowed to rival the illustrious men of Plutarch: Theseus, Lycurgus, Solon, and Caesar.'[48] The parallel lives of worthy personages could be used in an attempt to revive courtly values, though this must have been something of an anachronism in England by 1657, six years after the end of the Civil War.

So it was the turbulent period of the English Revolution that provided the setting for a totally unexpected re-emergence of a Thevetian portrait. Considerable use was made of accounts of ghosts, apparitions, miraculous events, witches and witchcraft, ancient prophecy, popular heroes, master criminals, sects and religious cults, monsters and peculiar natural occurrences in the propaganda wars waged in the news-books and pamphlets produced between 1640 and 1660. For instance, the birth of a hermaphrodite with neither nose, arms, legs nor hands, or of a monstrous kitten with eight feet, two tails, no head and paws like the hands of a child could be taken as an indication that the conflict between King Charles and Parliament was sinful indeed and that God had turned Nature upside down to repay those who would overturn the monarchy.[49] Around 10 per cent of newspaper stories during the interregnum were about monsters and portents;[50] whether they were born to Anglicans or Puritans depended on the political and religious persuasions of the pamphleteers. Either way, they were always a sign that the times were out of joint[51] and could therefore be cited as evidence that God was displeased with the current state of affairs.

This was the background against which a pamphlet was printed in London in 1653 called, as so many of them were, *The Wonder of our times*. It purported to be:

… a true and exact relation of the Body of a mighty Giant dig'd up at Brackford Bridge neer Ipswich in Suffolk, this present November 1651. his height 10 foot, his Head as big as half a bushell; with a description of the severall parts of his body, and manner of his interring. Certified in a Letter from a Gentleman in the Country, to his Brother (a merchant) in London.

Below this text, we see – the head of Atahualpa taken from Thevet's *Les Vrais Pourtraits et Vies* (illus. 85)![52] How this image came into the publisher's hands is a mystery, because the pamphlet antedates the publication of the illustrated edition of Plutarch's *Lives* by six years. At any rate, it is clear that the publisher can hardly have had any idea of its source in an Aztec codex: the image had wandered far outside of historical bounds.

It is interesting to note, however, that, though the publisher is unlikely to have been aware of it, there was a line of thought which linked America with gigantism, whether this was taken negatively to refer to the archaic and monstrous character of its inhabitants, or

The Wonder of our times:

BEING

A true and exact Relation of the Body of a mighty Giant
dig'd up at *Brockford* Bridge neer *Ipswich* in *Suffolk*, this present *November* 1651. his height 10.foot,his Head as big as half a bushell; with a description of the severall parts of his body, and manner of his interring.

Certified in a Letter from a Gentleman in the Country,to his Brother (a merchant)in *London*.

London : Printed by R. *Austin*, for *Wiley*, at PAUL's Chain. 1651.

85 Title page with vignette from *The Wonder of our times* (London, 1653).

positively to refer to the intact youth of a continent where the slow process of decay had scarcely begun.[53] Moreover, this is not the only instance of conflicts during the English Civil War being fought out at the allegorical level through a contrast between the Old World and the New: in Abraham Cowley's *Plantarum libri VI*, a didactic poem written in the years immediately following the Restoration, a competition between the trees of the Old and New worlds, leading to a quarrel between Bacchus and the Mexican god of wine, is perhaps intended to refer to the settlement of the Civil War with the return of Charles II and the reconciliation between King and Parliament.[54]

Dynastic troubles of a different kind formed the background to the resurgence of Thevetian imagery in the 1700s. Various portraits of early Andean rulers were utilized in the last quarter of the eighteenth century as part of claims by various noble families to be the rightful descendants of the Inca. Among these families was that of Diego Betancur Tupac Amaru, whose family archive in Cuzco contains an interesting European engraving, identified by an inscription as Felipe Tupac Amaru (killed in 1572), the last descendant of the Inca dynasty to head the resistance to the Spanish conquest in the sixteenth century. However, the portrait is not of Felipe Tupac Amaru; it can be identified as that of Atahualpa in chains, apparently directly copied from Thevet's woodcut.[55] This example shows the *generic* nature of these portraits, or at least the generic way in which they were treated – if one needed a portrait of an Inca, one regal figure was as good as another.[56]

It is as art in the service of politics that we can trace yet another re-emergence of images deriving from the *Codex Mendoza*, this time in the work of the twentieth-century Mexican muralist Diego Rivera. Among the frescoes which Rivera painted for the Cortés Palace, Cuernavaca, in 1930 is a scene of the battle for that town between Aztecs and Spaniards in April 1521. One of the Aztec warriors, dressed as an eagle, hurls a stone from a sling; he holds a blue and white shield with insignia dotted with black circles (the shield of the sun and warrior god Huitzilopochtli). This figure has been identified with the Eagle Knight (*quauhtín*) named, but not illustrated, in the *Codex Mendoza*,[57] although for a pictorial parallel one has to turn to another work, the so-called *Codex Florentino*, or to three-dimensional works like the earthenware Eagle Warrior excavated in the Templo Mayor in Mexico City.[58] Another Indian warrior in the fresco who is victorious over a Spaniard in armour can be identified as the Ocelot Knight. The battle standards surmounted by a coyote head that are borne by the Indian warriors are taken from folio 21v of the *Codex Mendoza*. A number of these warriors can be found in the even more ambitious stairway murals which Rivera subsequently painted in the Palacio National in Mexico City (illus. 86), while the depiction of people engaged in a number of practical activities, such as grinding corn on a grinding stone (*metatl*) or weaving at a loom, are also matched by scenes of children learning crafts in the *Codex Mendoza*

86 Diego Rivera, *History of Mexico: From the Conquest to the Future. North Wall: The Aztec World*, 1929, fresco. Palacio Nacional, Mexico City.

(illus. 87).[59]

This return of images from the *Codex Mendoza* to Mexico, almost four hundred years after their original creation, was mirrored in Rivera's own movements. Born there in 1886, he associated with Cubist painters in Paris and spent almost a year and a half studying Etruscan, Byzantine and Renaissance art in Italy before returning to Mexico in 1921. He studied the codices and chronicles, taking great care to authenticate every detail of his murals on the basis of exact research,[60] stimulated by the archaeological discoveries being made at the time. He was closely associated with the archaeologist Alfonso Caso, and from around 1930 began amassing a vast collection of pre-Columbian objects. Eventually, he had an Aztec-style pyramid temple (designed by Juan O'Gorman) built to house what had reached a total of almost 60,000 artefacts, and made Caso adviser to the collection and the building.

Given this background, it is clear that Rivera's use of the *Codex*

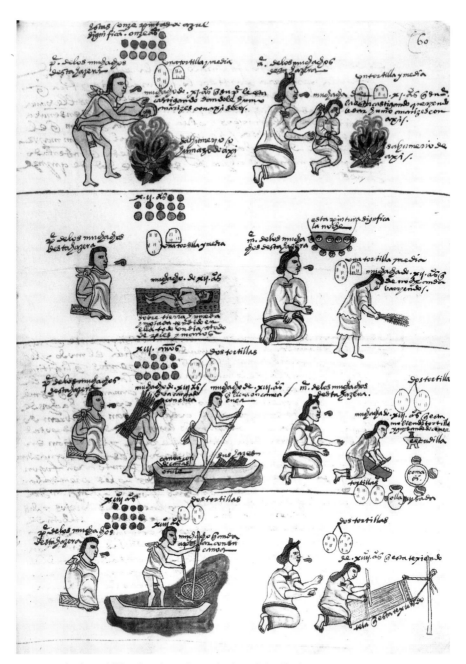

87 Aztec children learning various tasks, from *Codex Mendoza*.

Mendoza was by no means uninformed. It appears to have been one of his main sources, along with the *Lienzo de Tlaxcala* (a pictographic work on cloth painted around 1550 and now only known from copies, depicting moments of the conquest in which the Tlaxcalans appear as allies of the Spaniards) and the *Codex Florentino*. We can note his preference for post-conquest codices, which showed a measure of European influence, over less accessible codices of the earlier period. As a result of his use of more than one codex, as well as the influence of archaeological objects, Rivera created a Mesoamerican universe from images drawn from disparate times and places.[61] This is, of course, a long way from the geographical vagueness which we detected in the *Wunderkammern* and in sixteenth-century writers like Thevet and Montaigne. Since Rivera's use of his sources was a creative one, there was no need for him to draw slavishly on a single source, but there were limits to the degree of combination and conflation that he practised. After all, the political focus of his work was on a specific indigenous culture.

As we have seen, a significant feature of the sixteenth-century *Wunderkammern* was the detachment of the curiosities on display from their historical and cultural contexts. Rivera, on the contrary, in an effort to recreate an autonomous native American aesthetic, sought to restore what had been fragmented. As for the aristocratic filter, this too was turned upside down in Rivera's promotion of a revolutionary ideology. Both his collection and his paintings reveal an overall emphasis on the art and life of common people, even if his relationship to them (in this respect, his work is very different from that of his artist wife, Frida Kahlo) always seemed to be that of an outsider.[62]

Finally, in the use of the *Codex Mendoza* by Thevet's artist and his successor, we noted a tendency to Europeanize: facets that were difficult to grasp or portray were absorbed into a European aesthetic to make them more readily comprehensible. In the case of Rivera, the opposite process was at work. In his collection, the 'European' may be said to have been absorbed by the 'primitive'. In his painting, a clear example of this tendency can be seen in the Cuernavaca murals. In addition to drawing on codices, Rivera made use of the battle scenes by the Florentine Renaissance painter Paolo Uccello, whose work he had studied during his trip to Italy, but Uccello's aesthetic was absorbed within a self-conscious *indigenista* aesthetic.[63]

To recapitulate the tortuous trajectory which we have been considering, it is thanks to Joppien's demonstration of the dependence of Thevet's artist on images in the *Codex Mendoza* that we are able to trace the migrations of those images far from their Mexican origins. They surfaced in illustrations to Plutarch's *Lives*; they were used in the propaganda of the English Civil War; they played a role in Andean dynastic controversies around the time of the revolt of Tupac Amaru II; and in the 1930s, they re-entered Mexico within a different ideological framework to further the cause of the Mexican Revolution. Though they passed through various hands, Diego Rivera is probably the only one to have understood very much of what they meant in their native context; the level of Thevet's comprehension of the content of the *Codex Mendoza*, even with the aid of glosses, cannot have been all that high, and it may be assumed to have been non-existent on the part of the seventeenth-century London publishers who recycled the image of Atahualpa in their political pamphleteering. Leaving most of those who saw them 'in the dark', the images from the *Codex Mendoza* can truly be said to have led a life of their own.

Several of the names and other details encountered above recur in the micro-history of another codex, the *Codex Badianus*. This codex is the work of an Indian convert priest called Juan Badiano, who compiled and translated it into Latin from a 63-folio manuscript originally written in Tlateloco around 1552 by another Indian convert priest, Juan de la Cruz. The resulting syncretistic work, combining Renaissance representation with pre-Hispanic canons,[64] was dedicated and presented to Viceroy Mendoza and subsequently given to the Spanish King, Philip II. By the beginning of the seventeenth century, it was being kept in the library of Diego Cortavila y Sanabria, a physician in Madrid who also had a botanical garden. An entry in the diary of Cassiano dal Pozzo for 23 June 1626 refers to a visit by Cardinal Barberini and his retinue to this garden. On this occasion, the physician presented the cardinal with 'un Libretto di Semplici diversi Indiani con le sue figure, e virtù appropriate alla maggior parte dell'Indispositioni de' Corpi humani'.[65] The *Codex Badianus* was thus taken to Rome, where it continued to arouse the interest of the circle of scholars associated with the Accademia dei Lincei. Cassiano dal Pozzo had a copy made in the winter of 1626–7, by Vincenzo Leonardi da San Gimignano;[66] this 39-folio work is in fact as close to a facsimile as one could get before the age of mechanical reproduction, even reproducing the sixteenth-century hand of the original. The *Codex Badianus* and Cassiano dal Pozzo's 'quasi-facsimile' were accessible to only a few. However, the work reached a wider audience after it had been utilized as a source for the Mexican flora that accompanied illustrations of Mexican fauna in Johann Faber's *Animalia Mexicana descriptionibus scholijsque exposita…*, published in Rome in 1628. Faber

88 Diego Rivera, *The History of Medicine in Mexico: The People's Demand for Better Health*, 1953, fresco. Hospital de la Raza, Mexico City.

adhered closely to the Aztec originals, displaying the concern for documentary accuracy that is characteristic of the natural-history drawings in dal Pozzo's 'Paper Museum' as a whole.[67]

In 1953, Diego Rivera completed a mural for the Hospital de la Raza in Mexico City, *The People's Demand for Better Health* (illus. 88), in which he gave equal space to the portrayal of modern medicine and of Aztec medical practices. The dominant image in this mural is that of the fertility goddess Tlazolteotl, taken from the *Codex Borbonicus*, but beneath this goddess of physicians, midwives and healers, Rivera included a panel illustrating the variety of plants used medicinally by Aztec healers, all meticulously copied from the *Codex Badianus*.[68] Thus, having travelled from Mexico through Madrid to Rome, the Aztec images finally returned home.

5 Images and Objects

The starting point for the previous chapter was the *Codex Mendoza*, whose images we followed in their travels to unexpected places and times. The reverse process will be followed in the present chapter: beginning with composite images, we will unravel the stratification of their different source material. Some of that source material lies embedded in the pictorial images of the screen-folds discussed in Chapter 4, but other elements will prove to have their origins in three-dimensional objects and their representations.

It is important to bear in mind that many of the codices under discussion in this and the previous chapter were kept in collections of curiosities amid other exotic items. André Thevet, for instance, started to collect curiosities before he went to America. A trip to the Middle East in the winter of 1551 had furnished him with an ebony vase believed to have the power to counteract the effect of poison, as well as a 'serpent's tongue' or fossilized shark's tooth; among the Americana he took back to Paris were a Patagonian set of bow and arrows, a Brazilian toucan and a feathered head-dress of some kind.[1] It is therefore not surprising that a degree of promiscuity might have arisen between exotic images and exotic objects; this promiscuity left its mark on the lives of many images.

Close in time to Thevet's *Les Vrais Pourtraits et Vies* is the ceiling which Ludovico Buti decorated in the armoury of the Uffizi in Florence in 1588. The accurate depiction of birds from Central and South America in this ceiling probably reflects access to the Medici aviary, which included many exotic specimens. The family's collections also contained Mexican feather-work and carving, on which Buti could have drawn for some of the objects he painted.[2] However, if we examine the figure of an armed warrior on the ceiling, the inaccuracy of his shield (it resembles a Huaztec shield without the four crescents, but the way the feathers hang beneath it reveals a misunderstanding of their function) makes it hard to believe that the artist's source was an object he had actually seen; rather, it suggests an acquaintance with the shields depicted in the Aztec codices. The Medici possessed not only the *Codex Vindobonensis* and another book, the *Codex Magliabechiana*, but also the *Codex Florentino*.[3] Though the artist took certain liberties in adapting his sources, the animal skin, including the head, which the armed figure is wearing, as well as the standard behind his back, all recall figures like those in the *Codex Florentino*.[4] What is more, the way in which the Jaguar Warrior wears the animal skin in the codices was assimilated to the classical figure of Hercules, just as we saw in the case of Thevet's Paraousti Satouriona (see illus. 81).

The antiquary Lorenzo Pignoria (1571–1631) was the owner of a large collection in Padua that included paintings and prints, portraits of famous men, statues, coins, seals, ancient utensils, units of weight and measure, keys, clasps, rings, lamps, amulets, shells, stones, crystals and exotic objects from India and China.[5] Pignoria had the editorial responsibility for an illustrated text on the gods of Japan and Mexico that was included as an appendix to the edition of Vincenzo Cartari's *Le imagini colla sposizione degli dei degli antichi*, published in 1615. This iconographical work, compiled from a wide variety of (not equally trustworthy) sources by a protégé of the dukes of Ferrara called Vincenzo Cartari, contained a good number of 'barbarian' or pseudo-antique divinities as well as the better-established ones of Greco-Roman antiquity.[6]

As a member of an international network of intellectuals such as Nicolas-Claude Fabri de Peiresc, Pignoria had a wide variety of authorities on whom he could draw for advice and, when necessary, images. He himself stated that the images of Mexican gods in *Le imagini* were obtained through the mediation of Senator Ottaviano Malipiero from Cardinal Marco Antonio Amulio. It was probably while Amulio was occupying the position of Prefect of the Vatican Library in 1565–6 that he commissioned a number of drawings of foreign 'idols'. These coloured drawings on transparent paper are now in the Biblioteca Angelica, Rome, where they form part of MS 1551, entitled *Icones coloribus ornatae idolorum Mexicanorum*. A number of these drawings, which constitute the source for the woodcuts (by Filippo Ferroverde) of both Mexican and Japanese deities in Pignoria's appendix, were themselves copied from a Mexican codex, the 101-folio *Codex Vaticanus 3738*, also known as *Codex Vaticanus A* or *Codex Ríos*.[7] This book is regarded as a copy of the *Codex Telleriano-Remensis*, including the comments of Fray Pedro de los Ríos, made by an indigenous painter in Mexico in 1562. It is the only colonial Mexican manuscript to feature a lengthy, systematically composed Italian text to explain its images. From the fact that the commentary in the codex was written in Italian it is clear that the intention was to send it to Italy. It certainly entered the Vatican Library before 1600; the reference to Amulio, who died in 1570, would seem to indicate that this would have occurred soon after it had been completed, i.e. during 1565–6.[8]

Both the *Telleriano-Remensis* and the *Vaticanus A* codices contain mythological material, but the latter contains additional ethnographic and mythological sections not found in other ancient Mexican manuscripts, including the depiction of the Aztec cosmos with its thirteen celestial layers and nine levels of the underworld on the initial two facing folios. It was from the first of these that Pignoria took the god identified as Homoyoca (illus. 89). As insets he included two figures taken from the *Tabula Isiaca* (a first-century-AD Egyptianizing bronze table top of Campanian/Latian provenance excavated in

89 Filippo Ferroverde,
Woodcut showing the
god Homoyoca, from
Vicenzo Cartari, *Imagini
delli Dei de gl'Antichi*
(Venice, 1647).

Rome in 1527), on which he had written a commentary in 1605. Pignoria's four engravings of the infernal deities and their spouses (illus. 90, 91) were all taken from the same section of the *Vaticanus A*.

Although Pignoria's engravings are quite close to their model, they are sometimes hard to decipher without the support of the original. Thus, while it is not obvious what the object is in the lower right-hand corner of illustration 90, comparison with the original codex folio immediately makes it clear that the artist intended to depict the jaws of hell as the head of a monstrous, dragon-like creature, a widespread iconographical convention in Europe at least since the Middle Ages. Similar European models lie behind the representation of the divine messenger announcing the birth of Quetzalcoatl (illus. 92); the gesture of this figure replicates that of the angel Gabriel in scenes of the Annunciation.[9]

The wind god Quetzalcoatl himself was also depicted by Pignoria's artist (illus. 93); this figure is taken from folio 7v of the codex. Two discrepancies should be noted: neither the knot by which the god's cloak is fastened at the neck nor the cross on his incense burner are to be found in the original, even though Pignoria explicitly refers to the

90, 91 Ferroverde, Woodcut showing the infernal deities and their spouses, from Cartari, *Imagini* …

92 Ferroverde, Woodcut showing a divine messenger announcing the birth of the wind god Quetzalcoatl, from Cartari, *Imagini …*

cross in his text. Comparison with folio 14 of *Icones coloribus ornatae idolorum Mexicanorum* indicates that these additions originated in the drawings made from the codex for Cardinal Amulio.

In a revised edition of Cartari's *Le imagini colla sposizione degli dei degli antichi* printed by the same publisher in Padua in 1626, Pignoria added yet another image taken from *Codex Vaticanus A*: the god Quetzalcoatl (illus. 94), corresponding to folio 35r of the codex. Though taken from a section of the codex in which the deities represented are supposed to influence the fates of the days depicted (a divinatory almanac), Pignoria's artist divorced this deity from the thirteen-day segment which gave it its meaning. This process of detachment was not the work of Pignoria, however, for it had already been effected by the intermediary – in this case, identified as a certain Philippe de Winghe, who had taken the figure of the god from a 'Libro grande,

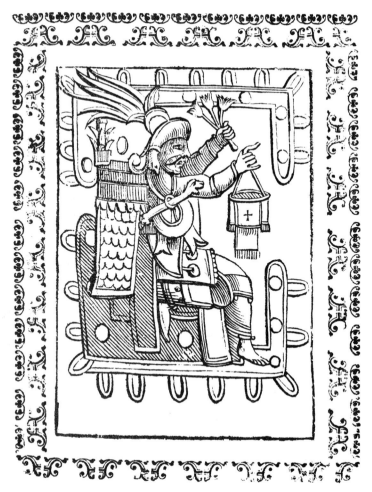

93 Ferroverde, Woodcut showing Quetzalcoatl, from Cartari, *Imagini ...*

ch'è nella Libreria Vaticana, compilato da F. Pietro de los Rios' – that is, *Codex Vaticanus A*. The Louvain-born artist Philip van Winghe (1560–1592) went to Rome, like many of his compatriots, in the second half of the sixteenth century to copy works of antiquity, an activity in which he was noted for accuracy as well as for skill in drawing. Van Winge, having played a pioneering role in the study of Christian archaeology, died of malaria in Florence in 1592.[10]

Pignoria's testimony regarding the transmission of images can be corroborated thanks to the preservation of another manuscript in the Biblioteca Angelica. MS 1564 is a book of sketches and drawings of inscriptions, reliefs, sarcophagi, statues and other antiquities in Rome, as well as portraits of popes and other personalities.[11] It is

94 Ferroverde, Woodcut showing another avatar of Quetzalcoatl, from Cartari, *Imagini* …

among this medley of representations – juxtaposed on the manuscript pages like objects in a *Wunderkammer* – that we find two coloured drawings of figures copied from *Codex Vaticanus A*: an Aztec warrior, taken from the ethnographic section of the codex (which did not interest Pignoria because he was concerned with divinities, not mortals), and the figure of Quetzalcoatl, taken from folio 35r.[12]

Pignoria concluded his section on Mexico with engravings of two American idols taken from yet another source. Based on drawings which he claimed to have received through the mediation of fellow Egyptologist Hans Georg Herwarth, they hark back to the contents of the *Kunstkammer* of the Duke of Bavaria in Munich. Mexico was well represented in this collection, one of the earliest of its kind north of the Alps; in 1575, Albrecht V wrote to Elisabeth of Valois, Queen of Philip II of Spain, asking her for exotic objects,[13] and the collection appears to have included Mexican hammocks, stone axes, feather-work and sculpture, as well as the Mixtec *Codex Vindobonensis I*.[14]

95 Ferroverde, Woodcut showing alleged parallels between Egypt and the Americas: Egyptian Horus and an idol from Florida, from Cartari, *Imagini* ...

Despite the presence of the Mixtec codex in the Bavarian collection, Pignoria's representations of two American idols derive from figures in the round. The first, the head illustrated on the left side of illustration 95, corresponds to an item listed in the 1598 inventory of the Munich collection as 'A wooden head of an idol from Florida. The neck black, the face yellow, across it a green line, the hair black, on it a broad wooden wreath, on the outside with small rosettes of untwined silk.' The central figure in this illustration, the god Horus, is Egyptian; Pignoria used these representations to support his

96 Ferroverde, Woodcut from Cartari, *Imagini* …

hypothesis that parallels between Mexico and Egypt proved that America had been conquered by the Egyptians.

The second figure in the round (illus. 96) appears in the 1598 inventory as 'An Indian idol on the outside covered with small white and red interlocking rings, with big eyes of blue glass'. (The red rings are clearly indicated in the coloured drawing on folio 4 of MS 1551.) It has been identified as a *zemi*, or idol, a class of icons regarded as the seats of supernatural beings by the Taino of the Greater Antilles. Once again, Pignoria's interest in the figure lay in the resemblance he perceived between it and the Egyptian Cercopithecus in the wood-cut's margin.[15]

Pignoria also adduced the use of hieroglyphics and the practice of mummification to demonstrate this alleged parallelism between Mexico and Egypt. Examining Indian and Japanese representations in the rest of the appendix to *Le imagini*, his purpose was the same: to demonstrate the Nilotic origins of Hindu temples and Japanese statues. In applying his findings to the comparative study of mythology and religion, Pignoria considered new discoveries seriously, not as picturesque curiosities.[16] This theoretical concern explains why he remained so faithful to his source. In his eyes, the figures taken from *Codex Vaticanus A* had documentary, not artistic, value; hence there could be no question of the use of artistic creativity to combine elements drawn from different contexts to produce composite portraits, as Thevet's artist had done in using the *Codex Mendoza*. Each of Pignoria's figures derived directly from its source; what was composite was the juxtaposition of images taken from different sources, both two- and three-dimensional.

In seeking to establish parallels between America and Egypt, Pignoria anticipated the activities of Alexander von Humboldt in the nineteenth century. Humboldt repeatedly compared Amerindian objects, such as pyramids, sculptural works or weapons, with parallels in ancient Greece, Italy and Egypt (the latter enjoyed particular popularity at this time as a result of the Napoleonic expedition there).[17] Humboldt made use of this comparison to bring out a contrast between American and European art, as can be seen from the frontal and dorsal representations of the bust of an 'Aztec priestess' in an engraving in his *Atlas of America* (1810). Humboldt compared this bust with ancient Egyptian and Greek sculpture, noting the care with which the toes were depicted; he interpreted the absence of hands as a sign that Amerindian art was still in its infancy – a view of such monuments as an intermediate stage between the 'childhood' of

97 Barthélemy-Joseph-Fuloran Roger after François Gérard, frontispiece to *Voyage de Humboldt et Bonpland* … (Paris, 1814–34), vol. 18.

humanity and 'true art' that was to be widely disseminated by Franz Kugler's extremely influential *Handbuch der Kunstgeschichte* (1841–2).[18] This view of native American art as 'infantile' harmonizes with Humboldt's view of South American nature as opening a window on the past. Indeed, given his theory of climatological determinism, the two are intrinsically related: the savagery of South American nature is reflected in the rudeness of native American art.

We find Humboldt's 'Aztec priestess' again, though upside down this time, in the frontispiece to Volume 18 of the *Voyage de Humboldt et Bonpland* (illus. 97).[19] This engraving was made after a drawing by the successful French artist François Gérard (1770–1837). Gérard, a pupil of David, rose to prominence after the display of his *Bélisaire* in the Salon of 1795, and was a popular figure among the Parisian intelligentsia.[20] By the time the *Voyage* was published, Humboldt was already aware of the importance of visualization to convey the impact of nature, having seen paintings of India by William Hodges, the first professional European landscape painter to portray the interior of northern India and a figure well known for his large canvases of the South Pacific.[21] Humboldt met Gérard during his second visit to Paris in 1798; their longstanding friendship is attested by the various portraits which the celebrated French painter made of his friend, by the fact that Humboldt worked for a time in Gérard's studio and attended his *soirées*, and by the correspondence which extended over a period of decades.[22]

Although the engraving appears as a frontispiece in Volume 18 of the 30-volume *Voyage*, a massive publishing undertaking that took 29 years to complete and is a bibliographer's nightmare, Humboldt already referred to it in the text to Volume 28, published in 1814 but without the frontispiece. According to Humboldt, the representation is of America consoled by Minerva and Mercury for the evils of the conquest. Gérard's original design bore the rubric 'L'Amérique relevée de sa ruine par le commerce et par l'industrie',[23] but the printed version has the caption 'humanitas, litterae, fruges', taken from a letter of Pliny the Younger describing how Greece had given civilization, the arts and wheat to other nations. America, Humboldt continued, was indebted to the Old World for these same benefits. He concluded by drawing attention to the faithful representation of weapons, clothing and monuments in the engraving.

The name 'America' for the figure on the left in the engraving does not make it clear whether we are to regard it as male or female, and its sex is not unequivocal. Most commentators have taken it to be male, referring to it as an 'Aztec prince'.[24] Personifications of the four continents tend to be female, however, which would lead one to expect this figure to be female too.

The artist drew on a variety of visual sources for the figure's clothing and accessories. Humboldt lent him a copy of his two-volume *Atlas pittoresque ou Vues des Cordillères et Monumens des peuples indigènes* (1810), which contained almost 70 engravings of native American ruins, codices and volcanic mountains. Humboldt used these to illustrate his thesis that the grandeur of the Andes and the Sierra Madre had acted as an environmental determinant on the forms of pre-Columbian civilizations. Thus, with minor modifications by the artist, we can trace America's shield, arrow, digging stick and tunic to three different warriors depicted in a codex which has become familiar to us from its use by Pignoria: *Codex Vaticanus A*. America's feathered headgear corresponds closely to an 'Aztec bas-relief' reproduced in the first plate of Humboldt's *Atlas pittoresque*. The upturned bust, represented as an 'Aztec priestess' in the *Atlas*, is based on a drawing of a basalt original, and was added to Gérard's composition by Humboldt himself. The decorations on the plinth derive from the Mitla Palace of the Columns, while the pyramid in the background is that of Cholula.[25]

This survey of the material reproduced in Humboldt's archaeological engravings and on which the artist of the frontispiece drew already indicates a paradox. While the need for accuracy in the depiction of native American artefacts is stressed by their careful, archaeologically authentic delineation, thereby conferring a degree of realism on the scene, the material itself was taken from a wide variety and diversity of sources. Aztec and Mixtec sources from different localities and periods are homogenized within the pages of the *Atlas pittoresque*. Torn from their times and places, they are juxtaposed in the frontispiece like the curiosities that filled the Renaissance *Kunst- und Wunderkammern*. Attention to realism here goes hand in hand with a failure to pay attention to the specificities of historical periods and local cultures. 'Pre-Columbian' they certainly are – but that is a wide term indeed.

One incongruous detail in America's costume does not look very pre-Columbian. This is the sandal painstakingly depicted on the figure's left foot, which looks remarkably Greek. The most obviously Greco-Roman elements of the frontispiece, however, are the female figure of Athena–Minerva, who bears an olive branch in her right hand, and the male figure of Hermes–Mercury, easily identifiable by the wand (*caduceus*) he carries in his right hand. The attributes of these two figures are largely conventional, corresponding to the iconography which had been established in handbooks for more than two centuries. These two readily identifiable Greco-Roman deities stand for the Old World, in opposition to the New World represented by America.

Besides the pre-Columbian and Greco-Roman elements, a third component calls for discussion: the representation of Chimborazo in the background. Why did the artist choose an *Andean* peak as the back-cloth to a predominantly *Mexican* scene? In 1802, Humboldt attempted to climb Mount Chimborazo, reaching an altitude of almost 6,000 m, only 400 m from the summit. At the time, Chimborazo was believed to be the highest mountain in the world, so Humboldt could justifiably claim that of all mortals he was the one who had risen highest in the world. In 1806, his friend Goethe drew a sketch showing Humboldt just below the summit of Chimborazo and Horace-Benedict de Saussure (the Swiss geologist and Alpine explorer) standing on top of Mont Blanc. Instead of the Atlantic Ocean, they are separated in Goethe's drawing by a stone slab bearing Humboldt's name. In other words, the significance of Humboldt's view from Chimborazo was that it offered a vantage point from which the whole globe could be contained and stratified. The New World could easily accommodate the Old, but not vice versa. It was not until 1822 that Humboldt's claim was shaken, when the Venezuelan revolutionary Simón Bolívar, literally following in his footsteps, became the first person to make it to the summit of Chimborazo. The personal link connecting Humboldt with the mountain is also apparent in the fact that this detail of the frontispiece derives from a sketch he made himself. The mountain appears in the frontispiece devoid of any setting, while the engraving in the *Atlas* includes the peak of Carguairazo as well. Chimborazo thus functions in the frontispiece as an icon for Humboldt himself and for the Humboldtian enterprise.

We have identified three iconographical strands in the Humboldt frontispiece: a pre-Columbian one, a Greco-Roman one and a personal one. The time has come to move from identification to interpretation. What effects are produced by the combination of these three strands within a single representation? Signification, according to a different Saussure, proceeds by way of distinctions. In the present case, then, which distinctions are imposed as significant, and what is *excluded* by the process of signification?

The closest compositional parallel to this frontispiece in Gérard's work is a drawing he made for the engraved illustrations to an edition of the *Aeneid* published in 1798. It is taken from Book VI, which describes Aeneas' journey to the underworld and his reunion with his father, Anchises, who serves as his guide there. There is a certain thematic appropriateness in this parallel, for the world of the pre-Columbian civilizations in the frontispiece is also a world of the dead. The figure of America is a museum piece situated among ruins. This notion conforms with a predilection shared by most nineteenth-century travellers in South America, for whom 'the crumbling monuments of the Aztecs, Incas, and Mayas were of greater interest than living inhabitants'[26] – a tendency that continued to characterize the response to native American art and artists on the part of the New York avant-garde in the twentieth century[27] and that is reflected in contemporary programmes of modernization that 'folklorize forms of life and deplore the loss of old – thereby confining Indian cultures to the museum and the curio shop'.[28] In the course of the five years (1799–1804) that Humboldt and the French naturalist Aimé Bonpland spent travelling through Mesoamerica and the Andes, they were compelled to interact with the contemporary inhabitants of Mexico and the Andes on a daily basis to sustain themselves and their project, for food, shelter and transport. But there is no trace of these contemporary individuals in the frontispiece.[29] Instead, the native American depicted there is a ghost of the past. There is a striking parallel in the attitude of nineteenth-century English travellers in Rome:

Many of the most powerful Romantic engagements with Rome tended to eliminate or to marginalize contemporary Romans and to find solitude and space for imaginative engagement with the spirit of the city and its history. It was no accident, too, that Rome was a 'City of the Dead' (a phrase which Shelley overtly borrowed from Germaine de Staël) since Romantic writers were often more comfortable with cities when their animation, at the least, suspended.[30]

The effect of the frontispiece, then, is to hide from view the contemporaneity of these nineteenth-century travellers to South America and the peoples they encountered. The anthropologist Johannes Fabian, describing how ethnographers conceive the people under investigation as belonging to a different order – even in temporal terms – calls this 'the denial of coevalness'.[31] In the process, the native Americans in the frontispiece are both archaeologized and exoticized.

It is in the eye of the (Humboldtian) observer that the Greco-Roman deities acquire significance as well. After all, their relevance is solely justified in terms of Humboldt's vision of a parallel between the Old World and the New. It reinforces the archaeologization of the native Americans, implying a contemporaneity with the mythological deities of Greece and Rome rather than with the observer. The quotation from Pliny the Younger further reinforces this frame of reference: in comparing Greece's gifts of civilization, the arts and agricultural products to its neighbours with the gifts of Europe to America, the colonial relations linking the Old World to the New are obscured. The material wealth which Europe had been deriving from America for centuries is transmuted and sanitized into archaeological wealth.

It should already be clear how the third component in the iconography of the frontispiece – Mount Chimborazo – falls into place within the Humboldtian view. It establishes a relation of property – *his* volcanic peak – which detaches the mountain from its geographical setting in Ecuador and relocates it within Humboldt's archaeologized America. The upturned 'Aztec priestess' is also connected directly with Humboldt, for the original on which it is based, now in the British Museum, was owned by him. The other pre-Columbian artefacts in the engraving are also based on engravings that had passed through Humboldt's hands. Given this extremely close relationship between the objects shown and Humboldt's physical person, it becomes plausible to view the frontispiece as a kind of self-portrait of the man displayed through his works.[32]

The connection between a natural phenomenon – the volcano – and cultural phenomena – the pre-Columbian archaeological artefacts – was closer at Humboldt's time than it might seem to us today. Volcanoes, particularly in a state of eruption, were seen to contribute to the history of the earth in the same way that archaeological objects contributed to the history of its inhabitants. For this dual interest in antiquities and eruptions we might compare the activities of the British antiquary and diplomat Sir William Hamilton in Italy, where he served as British ambassador from 1764 to 1800. A 1996 British Museum exhibition on Hamilton's work bore the eloquent title *Vases and Volcanoes*.[33] A similar concern with volcanoes, though transposed to an Orientalist literary mode, can be found in the closing pages of William Beckford's *The Vision*. The superficiality of knowledge confined to the earth's surface is here contrasted with the profundity that results from acquaintance with the world that flourishes in the earth's caverns. The point where depth and surface meet, where refined spirits converse with 'the simple descendants of those former rulers of the West, the mighty Incas', is 'toward the extreme peak of Catopaxi'.[34] Closer in time and affinity to Humboldt is the North American landscape painter Frederic Church (1826–1900), regarded as the Humboldt of painters. Church's various depictions of Chimborazo, Cotopaxi and other active volcanoes made on his trips to South America in 1853 and 1857 were not just exercises in the Sublime; the visual details embodied theories about the emergence of the earth's crust.[35]

It was thus only logical for the appropriation of American nature to proceed hand in hand with that of the native American past. Appropriation also called for adaptation within the new context. Hence that which was being subsumed had to be incorporated within a new explicitly and emphatically European framework. This process can be seen at work in the famous engraving of Chimborazo, based on a drawing by Humboldt, on which the different botanical species to be found at different altitudes are inscribed. Devoid of human presence, Chimborazo is represented as a *tabula rasa* to be filled in by a plethora of European names. In Humboldt's drawing, native American human activity has been suppressed and the depopulated mountain re-inscribed with the letters of a European taxonomy.

Thus the Humboldt frontispiece displays the convergence of a number of mechanisms: depopulation, deterritorialization, archaeologization. In other words, the human population of Central America and the Andes was stripped of its lands, removed from the present and consigned to a rigid archaeological past coeval with ancient Egypt, Greece and Rome. Yet it would be unjustified, on the basis of the present analysis, to accuse Humboldt of collusion with the physical acts of depopulation and deterritorialization. Indeed, his radical political views shocked many of his more conservative contemporaries. We are concerned here with the *effects* of the frontispiece. As a representation, it inevitably stands for something else; it represents a creative process of presence and absence. The frontispiece constructs or invents a particular view of America, and its effect on the viewer, whatever the intentions and allegiances of Humboldt (or Gérard, for that matter) may have been, is to present nineteenth-century America as a continent marked by continuity rather than change, as an Old World rather than a New World. In making sense of that world, it does not interpret it (that is our job); it *makes* it. Even when presenting America as a world of the dead, the image has lost none of its own vitality.

References

Introduction

1 The most detailed study of this elephant and its images is S. Bedini, *The Pope's Elephant* (Manchester, 1997). See also S. Deswarte, *Ideias e Imagens em Portugal na Época dos Descobrimentos: Francisco de Holanda e a teoria da arte* (Lisbon, 1992), pp. 24–6; E. Bassani and W. Fagg, *Africa and the Renaissance: Art in Ivory* (New York, 1988), pp. 102–4, 235; E. Bassani, 'Raphael at the Tropics?', *Journal of the History of Collections*, X/1 (1998), pp. 1–8; E. Bassani, *African Art and Artefacts in European Collections 1400–1800* (London, 2000), pp. 292–6.

2 P. Mason, *Infelicities: Representations of the Exotic* (Baltimore, 1998) contains discussions of Eckhout and of the kidnapping and display of non-Europeans in Europe in chaps 3 and 6, respectively.

3 V. I. J. Flint, *The Imaginative Landscape of Christopher Columbus* (Princeton, 1992), pp. 109, 121.

4 R. Wittkower, *Allegory and the Migration of Symbols* (London, 1977), p. 14.

5 *Ibid.*, p. 16.

6 P. Mason, 'Lévi-Strauss in Tenochtitlán', *Boletín de Estudios Latinoamericanos y del Caribe* XLV (1988), pp. 101–11; Wittkower, *Allegory and the Migration of Symbols*, p. 25.

7 *Ibid.*, pp. 46–74.

8 *Ibid.*, p. 14.

9 For instance, Maud Bodkin's influential *Archetypal Patterns in Poetry: Psychological Studies of Imagination* was published in 1934.

10 Wittkower, *Allegory and the Migration of Symbols*, p. 96.

11 On Ligozzi and the other members of the *'bottega artistica' aldrovandiana*, see the seminal work of G. Olmi, *L'inventario del mondo: Catalogazione della natura e luoghi del sapere nella prima età moderna* (Bologna, 1992), pp. 61–91.

12 Wittkower, *Allegory and the Migration of Symbols*, p. 11.

13 G. Didi-Huberman, *Phasmes: Essais sur l'apparition* (Paris, 1998), p. 41; see *ibid.*, p. 114, and *idem, Ce que nous voyons, ce qui nous regarde* (Paris, 1992), p. 13.

14 Wittkower, *Allegory and the Migration of Symbols*, pp. 99–100.

15 Mason, *Infelicities*, p. 13. Compare the monographic treatment of Panofsky in G. Didi-Huberman, *Devant l'image* (Paris, 1990).

16 Wittkower explicitly refers to the debate between 'diffusionist' and 'spontaneous generationist' ethnologists in *Allegory and the Migration of Symbols*, pp. 10, 16. On Panofsky's subsuming of ethnography and ethnology to the interpretative project of iconography and iconology in his *Meaning in the Visual Arts* (Harmondsworth, 1970), pp. 57–8, see Mason, *Infelicities*, pp. 14–15; Didi-Huberman, *Devant l'image*, pp. 151ff.

17 A. Warburg, *The Renewal of Pagan Antiquity*, intro. K. W. Foster, trans.

D. Britt (Los Angeles, 1999), p. 702.

18 *Ibid.*, and see p. 567.

19 *Ibid.*, p. 558.

20 Delivered as a lecture in 1923 under circumstances which have since become famous, it was first published in English in an abridged form in the *Journal of the Warburg Institute* (1938–9). The text followed here is that contained in A. Warburg, *Images from the Region of the Pueblo Indians of North America*, trans. with interpretive essay by M. P. Steinberg (Ithaca, 1995).

21 Wittkower, *Allegory and the Migration of Symbols*, p. 27 n. 137 on the parallelism of snake and thunderbolt.

22 Warburg, *Images*, p. 4.

23 *Ibid.*, pp. 49–50.

24 In an article entitled 'Manual Concepts: A Study of the Influence of Hand-Usage on Culture Growth', published in *American Anthropologist* in 1892, ethnographer Frank Hamilton Cushing posits a similar tripartite series of stages from the biotic through the manual to the mental; see L. Dilworth, *Imagining Indians in the Southwest: Persistent Visions of a Primitive Past* (Washington, DC, 1996), p. 151. Since Warburg, on his own admission (*Images*, p. 19), owed his 'initiation into the psychology of the will to animal metamorphosis' to Cushing, 'the pioneering and veteran explorer of the Indian psyche', his tripartite scheme may have been derived from the insights of his predecessor in the Southwest.

25 See F. Egmond and P. Mason, *The Mammoth and the Mouse: Microhistory and Morphology* (Baltimore, 1997), pp. 60ff; for a critique of 'reading off', see P. Mason, 'Ethnography, Ethnology and Para-anthropology: Sextus Empiricus and Hellenistic Comparative Method', *Aufstieg und Niedergang der Römischen Welt* II, vol. 37, pt 5 (in press).

26 Dilworth, *Imagining Indians*, p. 21.

27 See S. Greenblatt, 'Filthy Rites', in his *Learning to Curse: Essays in Early Modern Culture* (London, 1990), pp. 59–79.

28 Dilworth, *Imagining Indians*, p. 30.

29 M. Gidley, *Edward S. Curtis and the North American Indian, Incorporated* (Cambridge, 1998), p. 73.

30 Dilworth, *Imagining Indians*, p. 22.

31 W. J. Rushing, *Native American Art and the New York Avant-Garde* (Austin, 1995), pp. 67–8; see W. H. Truettner, 'The Art of Pueblo Life', in C. C. Eldridge, J. Schimmel and W. H. Truettner, *Art in New Mexico, 1900–1945: Paths to Taos and Santa Fe*, exh. cat., National Museum of American Art, Washington, DC (New York, 1986), p. 82.

32 Warburg, *Images*, p. 44.

33 Examples abound. Wittkower, for instance, noted the religious twist given by a fifteenth-century medal to a pagan motto derived from the letters of Cicero: *Duce Virtute Comite Fortuna* (Virtue be my guide and Fortune my companion) became *Deo Duce Virtute Comite Fortuna Faven[te]*; *Allegory and the Migration of Symbols*, p. 101.

34 Warburg, *Images*, p. 596.

35 Didi-Huberman, *Phasmes*, pp. 35–46.

36 See, for example, the refined analyses in F. Bouza, *Imagen y propaganda: Capítulos de historia cultural del reinado de Felipe II* (Madrid, 1998).

37 Warburg, *Images*, p. 585. See his remarks on the use of images that lack aesthetic appeal (*ibid.*, p. 598).

38 See the critique of the 'neo-iconological cult of detail', represented by the figure of Carlo Ginzburg, in Didi-Huberman, *Phasmes*, pp. 76–98, and the same

author's critique of Ginzburg's suppression of the symptomatic model in 'The Portrait, the Individual and the Singular: Remarks on the Legacy of Aby Warburg', in N. Mann and L. Syson, eds, *The Image of the Individual: Portraits in the Renaissance* (London, 1998), pp. 165–88.

39 See the argument that a photograph can 'capture traces of the surface phenomenology of things that really do exist. Of course, the social or cultural *meaning* we attach to these photographic traces lies outside the image itself, in the larger verbal and visual (and often unstated) systems of signification and communication to which we relate it' (N. L. Stepan, *Picturing Tropical Nature* [London, 2001]), pp. 87–8.

40 See E. Edwards, 'Jorma Puranen – Imaginary Homecoming', *Social Identities* 1/2 (1995), pp. 317–22; *idem, Raw Histories* (Oxford, 2001), pp. 211–33.

41 The painting was bought by the Bergen Company in 1724 and presented to King Frederik IV in the following year. The entry in the 1737 inventory of the Royal Danish Kunstkammer runs: 'A large Painting of two life-sized Male Persons from Greenland, the first to leave that Country of their own free will, arriving in Denmark in 1724. The former named Kieperoch, 34 years of age, and the latter Pock, 22 years of age.' See *Etnografiske genstande i Det kongelige danske Kunstkammer 1650–1800*, ed. B. Dam-Mikkelsen and T. Lundbæk (Copenhagen, 1980), pp. 1–4, 13–15. For discussion of the wider issues involved in reproducing, or not reproducing, images of people on show, see M. Bal, *Double Exposures: The Subject of Cultural Analysis* (London, 1996), pp. 185–224, and P. Mason, 'No Show', in *Antropology* [sic] *of Difference: Essays in Honour of Professor Arie de Ruijter*, ed. E. van Dongen and S. van Londen (Utrecht, 1998), pp. 139–57.

42 Movements of this kind are well documented for the collection of the Elector of Saxony in Dresden in D. Syndram, *Die Schatzkammer Augustus des Starken: Von der Pretiosensammlung zum Grüne Gewölbe* (Leipzig, 1999).

43 P. Findlen, 'A Site of Encounter: The Emergence of the Science Museum', in L. Guzzetti, ed., *Science and Power: the Historical Foundations of Research Policies in Europe* (Luxemburg, 2000), p. 60.

1 The Lives (and Deaths) of Fuegians and Their Images

1 W. Collins, *The Black Robe* (Stroud, 1994), p. 108.

2 C. Feest, 'From North America', in W. Rubin, *'Primitivism' in Modern Art: Affinity of the Tribal and the Modern*, 2 vols, exh. cat., Museum of Modern Art, New York (1984), pp. 85–98, esp. pp. 87–9.

3 R. W. Flint, 'American Showmen and European Dealers: Commerce in Wild Animals in Nineteenth-Century America', in R. J. Hoage and W. A. Deiss, eds, *New Worlds, New Animals: From Menagerie to Zoological Park in the Nineteenth Century* (Baltimore, 1996), p. 106 n. 38.

4 W. H. Schneider, *An Empire for the Masses: The French Popular Image of Africa, 1870–1900* (Westport, CT, 1982), pp. 125–51.

5 Philippe, Prince d'Araucanie, *Histoire du royaume d'Araucanie (1860–1979)* (Paris, 1979). For a discussion of some of the implications of the articulation of seemingly minor figures with political events of national or international import, see F. Egmond and P. Mason, 'A Horse Called Belisarius', *History Workshop*, XLVII (1999), pp. 240–51. Prince Roland Bonaparte's photographs of Mapuche and Fuegians in the Jardin in the 1880s are reproduced and discussed in C. Baez and P. Mason, *En el Jardín* (Santiago de Chile, in press).

6 L. Renieu, *Histoire des théâtres de Bruxelles* (Paris, 1928), pp. 877–87.

7 *Journal de Bruxelles*, 22 February 1890.

8   Columbus's remarks are taken from C. Colón, *Textos y documentos completos* (Madrid, 1984), p. 31. The relevant passage in Martyr's *De Orbe Novo* is 1.2.11. See G. Eatough, *Selections from Peter Martyr* (Turnhout, 1998), pp. 242, 262.

9   See the surveys in P. Mason, *Infelicities: Representations of the Exotic* (Baltimore, 1998), pp. 110–30; B. Kirshenblatt-Gimblett, *Destination Culture: Tourism, Museums, and Heritage* (Berkeley, 1998), pp. 17–128; and, for their role in imperial geography, F. Driver, *Geography Militant* (Oxford, 2001), pp. 148ff.

10 H. Cortés, *Letters from Mexico*, trans. and ed. A. R. Pagden (London, 1972), pp. 110–11.

11 E. L. Bridges, *Uttermost Part of the Earth* (New York, 1949), pp. 237–8.

12 A. Pigafetta, *Magellan's Voyage: A Narrative Account of the First Circumnavigation*, trans. and ed. R. A. Skelton (New Haven, 1969), vol. 1, pp. 53–7.

13 V. Roeper and V. and D. Wildeman, 'De Magellaanse Compagnie: Amsterdammers en Rotterdammers in een reis om de wereld', *Amstelodamum* LXXXVII/1 (2000), pp. 1–8.

14 O. van Noort, *Beschryvinghe vande Voyagie, om den geheelen Werelt Cloot, ghedaen door Olivier van Noort ...* (Amsterdam, 1602). This incident is also mentioned in *Extract oft Kort Verhaal wt het groote Journael*, a summary account of the voyage that was published by Jan van Waesberghe within a month of Van Noort's return in August 1601.

15 B. J. Potgieter, *Wijdtloopigh verhael van tgene de vijf schepen (die int jaer 1598 tot Rotterdam toegherust werden / om door de Straet Magellana haren handel te drijven) wedervaren is ...* (Amsterdam, 1600). This source also corroborates Van Noort's massacre of Fuegians on Santa Marta.

16 C. de Pauw, *Recherches philosophiques sur les Américains* (Berlin, 1774), pp. XII–XIII, 289. De Pauw's conclusions on the absence of giants in Patagonia were rejected by almost all of his contemporaries; see J. Duvernay-Bolens, *Les Géants patagons: Voyage aux origines de l'homme* (Paris, 1995), pp. 220–21.

17 The fullest account of these events can be found in a monograph on the subject by A. Chapman in press. It is summarized in the same author's 'Breve resumen de la historia de los yamana desde fines del siglo XVI hasta nuestros días', in P. Mason and C. Odone, eds, *12 miradas: Ensayos sobre los Selk'nam, yaganes y kawésqar* (Santiago de Chile, 2001). See also J. Browne, *Charles Darwin: Voyaging* (London, 1995). For accounts of the different ethnic groups that once inhabited Tierra del Fuego – the Selk'nam (or Ona), the Haush, the Alakaluf (also known as the Kawésqar or Kalakwulup) and the Yaghan (or Yamana), see C. McEwan, L. A. Borrero and A. Prieto, eds, *Patagonia: Natural History, Prehistory and Ethnography at the Uttermost End of the Earth* (London, 1997), and Mason and Odone, eds, *12 miradas*.

18 C. Darwin, *Journal of researches into the natural history and geology of the countries visited during the voyage of HMS Beagle round the world, under the command of Captain Fitz Roy, RN,* 2nd edn [1845] (Ware, 1997), pp. 198–9.

19 *Ibid.*, p. 196. On the vicissitudes of Thomas Bridges's dictionary, see R. H. Moeller, 'The Case of the Wandering Dictionary', reproduced from the Buenos Aires *Standard* with a postscript as Appendix II in Bridges, *Uttermost Part of the Earth*, pp. 529–37.

20 J. R. Forster, *Observations Made During a Voyage Round the World*, ed. N. Thomas, H. Guest and M. Dettelbach (Honolulu, 1996), p. 171; Darwin, *Journal*, p. 203.

21 P. Revol, '1881 Des Fuégiens en Europe', in A. Chapman, C. Barthe and P. Revol, *Cap Horn, rencontre avec les Indiens Yahgan* (Paris, 1995), pp. 28–38.

22 P. Juillerat, 'Les Fuégiens du Jardin d´Acclimatation', *La Nature* (1881), pp. 295–8.

23 G. Eissenberger, *Entführt, verspottet und gestorben: Lateinamerikanische Völkerschauen in deutschen Zoos* (Frankfurt, 1996), pp. 107–10.

24 For instance, the 1881 edition of *La Nature*, which contained an article on the Fuegians in the Jardin by Paul Juillerat, also included an article, signed 'P.J.', on 'The Prairie Dogs in the Jardin d'Acclimatation' (2 July 1881, pp. 65–6), as well as articles on the exhibitions of dwarfs in other locations in the French capital, including 'An Extraordinary Dwarf: Princess Paulina in Paris' (19 March 1881, pp. 255–6).

25 On the movements and deaths of this group of Fuegians, see R. Brändle, *Wildfremd, hautnah: Völkerschauen und Schauplätze Zürich 1880–1960: Bilder und Geschichten* (Zurich, 1995), pp. 7–21; Eissenberger, *Entführt*, pp. 166–71; H. Thode-Arora, *Für fünfzig Pfennig um die Welt: Die Hagenbeckschen Völkerschauen* (Frankfurt, 1989), pp. 35, 97.

26 W. Haberland, 'Nine Bella Coolas in Germany', C. Feest, ed., *Indians and Europe: An Interdisciplinary Collection of Essays* (Aachen, 1987), p. 344.

27 R. Poignant, 'Surveying the Field of View: The Making of the RAI Photographic Collection', in E. Edwards, ed., *Anthropology and Photography 1860–1920* (New Haven, 1992), pp. 51–4.

28 Eissenberger, *Entführt*, pp. 166–71.

29 Julius Popper, cited in M. Gusinde, *Los Indios de Tierra del Fuego: I: Los Selk'nam* (Buenos Aires, 1982), p. 153. On Popper's role in the extermination of the Selk'nam, see C. Odone and M. Palma, 'La muerte exhibida fotografías de Julius Popper en Tierra del Fuego', in Mason and Odone, eds, *12 miradas*.

30 *South America Missionary Magazine* (1 November 1889), p. 240. This source also gives their number as nine.

31 *South America Missionary Magazine* (1 February 1890), p. 29.

32 *Journal de Bruxelles*, 6 February 1890.

33 This evidence is corroborated by a document in the Algemeen Rijksarchief Brussel (see S. Vervaeck, *Inventaire des archives du ministère de la justice: Administration de la sûreté publique [Police des étrangers]: Dossiers généraux* [1968], no. 834: Troupes d'étrangers exhibés en public. 1888–1904). Although the full dossier is missing, the description of contents refers to a 'Troupe of Ona exhibited in February 1890 in the Musée du Nord and who were returned to England'.

34 *South America Missionary Magazine* (1 March 1890), p. 53.

35 Gusinde, *Los Indios*, pp. 152–3 n. 179, mentions him as an interpreter for Father J. M. Beauvoir.

36 Haberland, 'Nine Bella Coolas', p. 368.

37 F. Bornemann, *P. Martin Gusinde (1886–1969): Mitglied des Anthropos-Institutes* (Rome, 1971), p. 12.

38 *Bulletin de la Société d'Anthropologie de Bruxelles*, VII (1888–9), p. 286.

39 *Bulletin de la Société d'Anthropologie de Bruxelles*, VIII (1889–90), pp. 241–55.

40 *Bulletin de la Société d'Anthropologie de Bruxelles*, IX (1890–91), p. 45.

41 F. Lahille, 'Matériaux pour servir à l'histoire des Oonas indigènes de la Terre de Feu', *Revista del Museo de la Plata*, XXIX (1926), pp. 339–61. Most of Lahille's article is taken up with fanciful etymologies intended to demonstrate that the Selk'nam were descended from the ancient civilizations of the Old World.

42 P. Revol, 'Hyades, anthropologue physique et ethnographe', in Chapman, Barthe and Revol, *Cap Horn*, pp. 98–9.

43 Schneider, *An Empire*, p. 132; L. A. Sánchez Gómez, 'Ethnographie, muséologie

et colonialisme dans l'Espagne de la fin du XIXe siècle: Le Musée-Bibliothèque d'Outre-mer (1888–1908)', in *Studium et Museum: Mélanges †Édouard Remouchamps* (Liège, 1996), pp. 814–15; and see P. Romero de Tejada, *Un templo a la ciencia: Historia del Museo Nacional de Etnología* (Madrid, 1992).

44 Lahille, 'Matériaux', explanation des planches.

45 C. Barthe, 'Les Omaha de Bonaparte: Exemples de photographie scientifique et de représentations iconographiques', in B. Coutancier, ed., *'Peaux-Rouges': Autour de la collection anthropologique du prince Roland Bonaparte* (Paris, 1992), p. 69.

46 *Ibid.*, pp. 70–73; see B. Coutancier, 'Découvrir l'Autre au Jardin d'Acclimatation: Exhibitions ethnographiques et vulgarisation scientifique (1877–1890)', in Coutancier, ed., *Peaux-Rouges*, pp. 39–46.

47 For his views on the Fuegians, see G. Le Bon, 'Les Fuégiens', *Bulletin de la Société de Géographie*, 7th ser., IV (1883), pp. 266–78.

48 See E. Edwards, 'Ordering Others: Photography, Anthropologies and Taxonomies', in C. Iles and R. Roberts, eds, *In Visible Light: Photography and Classification in Art, Science and the Everyday*, exh. cat., Museum of Modern Art, Oxford (1997), pp. 54–68.

49 On the penchant for presenting human subjects like hunting trophies, see Mason, *Infelicities*, pp. 122–3; Odone and Palma, 'La muerte exhibida'.

50 The photographic print and the postcard are reproduced in *Odagot: Photographs of American Indians 1860–1920*, exh. cat., Museum of Ethnology, Rotterdam (Amsterdam, 1992), p. 97. On 'doctoring', 'faking' and 'reconfiguring' photographs to create suitable postcard images, see P. C. Albers, 'Symbols, Souvenirs and Sentiments: Postcard Imagery of Plains Indians, 1898–1918', in C. M. Geary and V.-L. Webb, eds, *Delivering Views: Distant Cultures in Early Postcards* (Washington, DC, 1998), p. 70. More generally, see *Anthropology and Photography*; E. Edwards, *Raw Histories* (Oxford, 2001).

51 A. Wendt, *Kannibalismus in Brasilien* (Frankfurt, 1989), p. 164. On allegories of the four continents, see also Mason, *Infelicities*, pp. 106–8.

52 Pigafetta, *Magellan's Voyage*, p. 49.

53 A. Chapman, *Fin de un mundo* (Santiago de Chile, 2001), chap. 6.

54 See above, Introduction.

55 Pigafetta, *Magellan's Voyage*, p. 142. The artist's source has been located in two accounts of Magellan's voyage published in G. B. Ramusio, *Navigazioni e viaggi* (Venice, 1550); see A. Bettini, '"Americae Retectio": Ricostruzione di un processo creativo', *Columbeis*, III (1988), pp. 191–201.

56 They are taken from Potgieter's *Wijdtloopigh verhael van tgene de vijf schepen (die int jaer 1598 tot Rotterdam toegherust werden om door de Straet Magellana haren handel te drijven) wedervaren is …* (Amsterdam, 1600).

57 On this stereotype, see Mason, *Infelicities*, chap. 2. The various figures in these plates – the man with the harpoon, the woman feeding her children, the man in the feathered dress and the female survivor – all appear together in Volume 9 of De Bry's *Great Voyages* (1601).

58 For a development of this view, see P. Mason, *Deconstructing America: Representations of the Other* (London, 1990).

59 C. Feest, 'Tierra del Fuego/Feuerland', in B. Hauser-Schäublin and G. Krüger, eds, *James Cook: Gifts and Treasures from the South Seas: The Cook/Forster Collection, Göttingen* (Munich, 1998), pp. 264–7.

60 B. Smith, *European Vision and the South Pacific* (New Haven, 1985), p. 36; see R. Joppien and B. Smith, *The Art of Captain Cook's Voyages: Volume 1: The Voyage of the Endeavour 1768–1771* (New Haven, 1988), pp. 10–19.

61 B. Smith, *Imagining the Pacific: In the Wake of the Cook Voyages* (New Haven, 1992), p. 56.

62 Smith, in *ibid.*, inaccurately refers to them as 'a tribe of the Ona Indians of Patagonia', i.e. Selk'nam. The Haush occupied the south-eastern corner of Isla Grande.

63 These transformations are documented in Smith, *European Vision*, pp. 37–40, and *idem*, *Imagining*, pp. 59–62.

64 H. Honour, ed., *L'Amérique vue par l'Europe*, exh. cat., Grand Palais, Paris (1976), no. 298.

65 *Auguste Préault, sculpteur romantique 1809–1879* (Paris, 1997), no. 88; see also *La Sculpture ethnographique*, exh. cat., Musée d'Orsay, Paris (1994), no. 24.

66 G. Lacambre, 'Gustave Moreau et l'exotisme', in *Gustave Moreau 1826–1898*, exh. cat., Grand Palais, Paris (1998), pp. 23–7; see D. Kosinski, 'Picturing Poetry: Photography in the Work of Gustave Moreau', in *The Artist and the Camera: Degas to Picasso*, exh. cat., Dallas Museum of Art (New Haven, 1999), pp. 60–69.

67 Geneviève Lacambre, personal communication.

68 T. Gott, 'La Genèse du symbolisme d'Odilon Redon: Un nouveau regard sur le *Carnet de Chicago*', *Revue de l'Art*, XCVI (1992), pp. 51–62.

69 D. W. Druick *et al.*, *Odilon Redon: Prince of Dreams 1840–1916*, exh. cat., Art Institute of Chicaco, Royal Academy, London, and Van Gogh Museum, Amsterdam (New York, 1994), p. 140.

70 Redon's interest in native Americans was not confined to the southern continent. He was an admirer of the dreamlike work of Rodolphe Bresdin, who was inspired, as were so many others, by *The Last of the Mohicans*; for a representation that is closer to nightmare than dream, compare Bresdin's pen-and-wash *La Torture* (1850–70), showing native Americans from the north engaged in a gruesome torture; see Honour, ed., *L'Amérique vue*, no. 300.

71 *Remota: Pinturas Aeropostales: Eugenio Dittborn: Airmail Paintings*, exh. cat., New Museum of Contemporary Art, New York, and Museo Nacional de Bellas Artes, Santiago (Santiago, 1997); *Mundana, 24 pinturas aeropostales en el Museo Nacional de Bellas Artes de Santiago de Chile* (Santiago, 1998), p. 34.

72 *Luis F. Benedit en el Museo Nacional de Bellas Artes: Obras 1960–1996*, exh. cat., Museo Nacional de Bellas Artes, Buenos Aires (1996).

73 On the perpetual circulation of the peoples of Latin America and their images, see C. Merewether, 'The Migration of Images: Inscriptions of Land and Body in Latin America', in P. Vandenbroeck, ed., *America Bride of the Sun: 500 Years Latin America and the Low Countries*, exh. cat., Royal Museum of Fine Arts, Antwerp (1992), pp. 197–222; on the ongoing process of recontextualization, see Egmond and Mason, 'A Horse Called Belisarius'.

74 W. Parker Snow, *A Two Years Cruise off Tierra del Fuego, the Falkland islands, Patagonia and in the River Plate: a narrative of life in the Southern Seas* (London, 1857), vol. II, pp. 37–8. The portraits of Jemmy and the other Fuegians appeared in R. Fitz-Roy, *Narrative of the Surveying Voyages of his Majesty's ships 'Adventure' and 'Beagle' between the years 1826 and 1836, describing their examination of the southern shores of South America and the 'Beagle's' circumnavigations of the globe. Vol. I Proceedings of the First Expedition, 1826–1830, under the command of Captain P. Parker King; Vol. II Proceedings of the Second Expedition, 1831-1836, under the command of Captain Robert Fitz-Roy, R.N.* (London, 1839).

75 Chapman, 'Breve resumen'.

76 More information at http://www.cuerpospintados.com.

1   P. Mason, *Infelicities: Representations of the Exotic* (Baltimore, 1998), pp. 18, 46.

2   F. Egmond and P. Mason, '"These Are People Who Eat Raw Fish": Contours of the Ethnographic Imagination in the Sixteenth Century', *Viator*, XXXI (2000), pp. 311–60. Coenen's manuscripts are discussed in F. Egmond and P. Mason, *The Mammoth and the Mouse: Microhistory and Morphology* (Baltimore, 1997), pp. 23–36. There are both black-and-white and colour illustrations from them in F. Egmond, *Een bekende Scheveninger: Adriaen Coenen en zijn Visboeck van 1578* (Scheveningen, 1997).

3   *Histoire Naturelle des Indes: The Drake Manuscript in the Pierpont Morgan Library* (New York, 1996). See F. Lestringant, *L'Experience huguenote au nouveau monde (XVIᵉ siècle)* (Geneva, 1996), pp. 265–90. For the importance of these sources for 'the view from below', see P. Mason, 'Figures of America', *Eighteenth-Century Life*, XX (1996), p. 115.

4   The same subject matter features in one of the earliest visual sources for the New World: the marginal sketches in the so-called Ferrara Manuscript; see L. Laurencich-Minelli, *Un 'giornale' del Cinquecento sulla scoperta dell'America: Il Manoscritto di Ferrara* (Milan, 1985).

5   W. C. Sturtevant, 'First Visual Images of Native America', in F. Chiappelli, ed., *First Images of America* (Berkeley, 1976), vol. I, p. 419.

6   See P. Mason, 'Eighty Brazilian Birds for Johan Georg', *Folk* (in press).

7   The recent facsimile edition, *Brasil-Holandês / Dutch Brazil* (Rio de Janeiro, 1995), only reproduces those pages of the *Miscellanea Cleyeri* relating to Brazil, and thus omits the two pages reproduced here, which gives a misleading picture of the contents of the volume as a whole.

8   A. B. Smith and R. H. Pheiffer, *The Khoikhoi at the Cape of Good Hope: Seventeenth-century Drawings in the South African Library* (Cape Town, 1993). Basic for the study of the iconography of the Khoikhoi is E. Bassani and L. Tedeschi, 'The Image of the Hottentot in the Seventeenth and Eighteenth Centuries', *Journal of the History of Collections*, II/2 (1990), pp. 157–86.

9   Lambeth Palace Papers, No. 6, MS 954, item 27. The drawings are pasted onto six sheets and are completely heterogeneous among the collection of letters and other documents relating to church affairs. Poor-quality reproductions of three of them ('Rusticus', 'Sponsa' and 'Vice Regina') appear in F. J. Foley, *The Great Formosan Impostor* (Taipei, 1968).

10 George Psalmanaazaar, *An Historical and Geographical Description of Formosa* (London, 1704), p. 227.

11 *Ibid.*, p. 230.

12 *Ibid.*, p. 228.

13 *Ibid.*, p. 230.

14 *Ibid.*, p. 232.

15 *Ibid.*

16 *Ibid.*

17 Foley, *The Great Formosan Impostor*, p. 17 n. 5.

18 George Psalmanaazaar, *Memoirs of ****: Commonly known by the name of George Psalmanazar; A Reputed Native of Formosa* (London, 1764), p. 172.

19 Foley, *The Great Formosan Impostor*, p. 17. For what it is worth, the authors of an anonymous *Enquiry into the Objections against George Psalmanaazaar of Formosa* ... dating from around 1710 report that 'Ps—r tells us he gave only general Directions to the Engraver, who added some Ornaments to the Habits' (*ibid.*, p. 35).

20 On these collections, see D. Defert, 'Les Collections iconographiques du XVIᵉ

siècle', in J. Céard and J.-C. Margolin, eds, *Voyager à la Renaissance: Actes du colloque de Tours 1983* (Paris, 1987), pp. 531–43.

21 For this iconography, see S. Moser, *Ancestral Images: The Iconography of Human Origins* (Stroud, 1998).

22 For a detailed analysis of the iconography of the engravings in Linschoten's work, see E. van den Boogaart, *Superior and Corrupt Asia* (Chicago, in press).

23 Psalmanaazaar, *An Historical and Geographical Description*, pp. 1–37, 37–144, and 145–327, respectively.

24 J. de Léry, *Histoire d'un voyage faict en la terre du Bresil, autrement dite Amerique* (Geneva, 1578).

25 Psalmanaazaar, *An Historical and Geographical Description*, fig. 6, p. 224.

26 Mason, *Infelicities*, p. 44.

27 Psalmanaazaar, *An Historical and Geographical Description*, fig. 3, p. 194.

28 The anthropologist R. Needham, in *Exemplars* (Berkeley, 1985), p. 105, is sceptical about the influence of these theories on Psalmanazaar: 'Nothing that we know of Psalmanazaar's life makes it all likely, or even very possible, that he should have been acquainted with these or other such works.' In view of the paucity of our knowledge about the man himself, however, it would be rash to deny the possibility of his having been influenced by them. See J. Stagl, *A History of Curiosity: The Theory of Travel 1550–1800* (Chur, 1995) p. 181 n. 18.

29 On attempts by Irish antiquarians to link the Gaelic language and Celtic culture to the Phoenicians, the Etruscans and China, see J. T. Leerssen, *Remembrance and Imagination* (Cork, 1996), pp. 70ff.

30 See P. Cornelius, *Languages in Seventeenth- and Early Eighteenth- Century Imaginary Voyages* (Geneva, 1965), pp. 39ff.

31 For this and other examples of the conflation of the inhabitants of the Americas with aliens from outer space, see J. Adams, 'Outer Space and the New World in the Imagination of Eighteenth-Century Europeans', *Eighteenth-Century Life*, XIX (1995), pp. 70–83.

32 W. Empson, *Essays on Renaissance Literature: Donne and the New Philosophy: Vol. I* (Cambridge, 1993), pp. 220–54.

33 One might compare the versions of the Lord's Prayer and the Apostles' Creed in the philosophical language devised by John Wilkins in his *Essay toward a Real Character and Philosophical Language* (1668); see Cornelius, *Languages*, pp. 93–6.

34 E. Cohen, 'Symbols of Culpability and the Universal Language of Justice: The Ritual of Public Executions in Late Medieval Europe', *History of European Ideas*, XI (1989), pp. 407–16.

35 Psalmanaazaar, *An Historical and Geographical Description*, p. 164.

36 F. Lestringant, ed., *Le Brésil d'André Thevet: Les Singularités de la France Antarctique (1557)* (Paris, 1997), p. 243. The woodcut accompanying this passage was re-used in Thevet's *Cosmographie universelle* (1575), fol. 960v with the title 'Cruauté de ces femmes guerrières'. For further discussion of this passage, see P. Mason, 'Continental Incontinence: *Horror vacui* and the Colonial Supplement', in R. Corbey and J. T. Leerssen, eds, *Alterity, Identity, Image. Selves and Others in Society and Scholarship* (Amsterdam, 1991), pp. 151–90.

37 2 Kings 17:3.

38 Lestringant, ed., 'Introduction', in *Le Brésil*, p. 25.

39 See P. Mason, 'Classical Ethnology and Its Influence on the European Perception of the Peoples of the New World', in W. Haase and M. Reinhold, eds, *The Classical Tradition and the Americas, vol. I, pt. 1: European Images of the Americas and the Classical Tradition* (Berlin and New York, 1994), pp. 135–72.

40 Ambroise Paré, for example, situated it in Africa in his *Des Monstres et Prodiges* (Paris, 1573).

41 Psalmanaazaar, *An Historical and Geographical Description*, p. 265.

42 Needham, *Exemplars*, pp. 107–13; for a fuller discussion of analogical classification, see his *Reconnaissances* (Toronto, 1980), pp. 63–105.

43 Jean de Léry, *Histoire d'un voyage fait en la terre du Brasil 1557*, ed. F. Lestringant (Montpellier, 1992), pp. 149–50; M. de Montaigne, *Des Cannibales*. See too the discussion by C. Rawson, 'Savages Noble and Ignoble: Natives, Cannibals, Third Parties, and Others in South Pacific Narratives by Gulliver, Bougainville, and Diderot, With Notes on the *Encyclopédie* and on Voltaire', *Eighteenth-Century Life*, XVIII (1994), pp. 168–97, esp. 184–8.

44 Psalmanaazaar, *An Historical and Geographical Description*, p. 224.

45 Psalmanaazaar, *Memoirs of *****, p. 135.

46 F. Lestringant, 'Travels in Eucharistia: Formosa and Ireland from George Psalmanaazaar to Jonathan Swift', *Yale French Studies*, LXXXVI (1994), pp. 109–25. For an extended version of this article, see the chapter 'Formose et l'Irlande' in his *Une sainte horreur, ou le voyage en Eucharistie XVIᵉ-XVIIIᵉ siècle* (Paris, 1996), pp. 311–30.

47 Psalmanaazaar, *An Historical and Geographical Description*, p. 251.

48 *Ibid.*, pp. 181, 188.

49 *Ibid.*, p. 235. On the invention of home-made yardsticks for measuring and comparing, see A. Maczak, 'Renaissance Travellers' Power of Measuring', in J. Céard and J.-C. Margolin, eds, *Voyager à la Renaissance: Actes du colloque de Tours 1983* (Paris, 1987), pp. 245–56.

50 Lestringant, 'Travels in Eucharistia', p. 111, describes the holy terror of the bloody sacrifice as 'distanced from the reader and adorned with a glamour of exoticism'.

51 H. H. H. Remak, 'Exoticism in Romanticism', *Comparative Literature Studies*, XV/1 (1978), p. 60; see P. Mason, 'On Producing the (American) Exotic', *Anthropos*, XCI (1996), pp. 139–51.

52 Psalmanaazaar, *Memoirs of *****, p. 70.

53 *Ibid.*, p. 172.

54 Various first names (George, William) are provided in the secondary literature. Foley, *The Great Formosan Imposter*, p. 11, has established Alexander as the correct name on the basis of archival evidence.

55 Psalmanaazaar, *Memoirs of *****, pp. 138–9.

56 *Ibid.*, p. 56.

57 On autobiographical discourse as a discourse of self-restoration, and on the unresolved nature of the distinction between autobiography and fiction, see P. de Man, *The Rhetoric of Romanticism* (New York, 1984), pp. 67–81.

58 Foley, *The Great Formosan Imposter*, pp. 58–65.

59 See T. Todorov, *Les Morales de l'histoire* (Paris, 1991), pp. 129–41.

60 Foley, *The Great Formosan Imposter*, p. 92.

61 See S. Stewart, 'Antipodal Expectations: Notes on the Formosan "Ethnography" of George Psalmanazar', in G. W. Stocking Jr, ed., *Romantic Motives: Essays on Anthropological Sensibility* (Madison, 1989) pp. 44–73. One could compare this predicament with the one faced by Guaman Poma de Ayala of 'how to cast the narrator as the trustworthy confidant whose very authority derives from his condition of exotic strangeness'; see R. Adorno, *Guaman Poma: Writing and Resistance in Colonial Peru* (Austin, 1986), p. 131.

62 R. A. Day, 'Psalmanazar's "Formosa" and the British Reader (including Samuel Johnson)', in G. S. Rousseau and R. Porter, eds, *Exoticism in the Enlightenment*

(Manchester, 1989), p. 207. In later life, after he had given up his role as a Formosan impostor, Psalmanaazaar made use of the short account of Formosa by the Dutch missionary George Candidius, though with the proviso that 'this will be found to deserve as little Credit, as that of our pretended Formosan' (cited in Foley, *The Great Formosan Imposter*, p. 55).

63 M. Jones, ed., *Fake? The Art of Deception*, exh. cat., British Museum, London (1990).

64 J. A. Farrer, *Literary Forgeries* (London, 1907); P. G. Adams, *Travelers and Travel Liars 1660–1800*, 2nd edn (New York, 1980).

65 S. Bann, *The Clothing of Clio: A Study of the Representations of History in Nineteenth-Century Britain and France* (Cambridge, 1984), p. 2 (Bann goes on to list Macpherson's *Ossian*, Chatterton's medieval poetry and Charles Bertram's forged *Chronicle of Sirhcrad of Cirencester*, the latter published in 1757 and republished as authentic in 1878!).

66 E. Morpurgo, 'Anche nel 1704 Formosa era all'ordine del giorno', *Rivista degli studi orientali*, XXXII (1957), p. 759.

67 W. Campbell, *The articles of Christian instruction in Favorlang-Formosan, Dutch and English* (London, 1896).

68 See, for instance, the watercolours and sketches by Aron from Kangeq, the 'father of Greenland painting', in B. Kaalund, ed., *Aron fra Kangeq 1822–1869* (Copenhagen, 1997); K. Thisted, ed., *Således skriver jeg Aron: Samlede fortællinger og illustrationer af Aron fra Kangeq (1822–1869)*, 2 vols (Nuuk, 1999).

69 M. Lefevre, 'Bibliothèques et lecteurs à la Bastille au XVIIIᵉ siècle', *Bulletin du bibliophile*, II (1994), pp. 333–68. The best modern edition of *Aline et Valcour* is in D. A. F. de Sade, *Oeuvres I* (Paris, 1990). On Sadean 'para-ethnography', see F. Egmond and P. Mason, 'Domestic and Exotic Cruelties: Extravagance and Punishment', *Irish Review*, XXIV (1999), pp. 31–52.

70 W. Collins, *Ioláni; or, Tahiti as it was. A Romance*, ed. I. B. Nadel (Princeton, 1999). The editor's introduction contains a detailed account of Collins's use of Ellis and other sources.

3 From America to Oxfordshire?

1 W. C. Sturtevant, 'First Visual Images of Native America', in F. Chiappelli, ed., *First Images of America* (Berkeley, 1976), vol. 1, p. 420.

2 *Ibid.*, p. 419.

3 *Ibid.*, p. 424. See J. Carrillo, 'Taming the Visible: Word and Image in Oviedo's *Historia General y Natural de las Indias*', *Viator*, XXXI (2000), pp. 399–431, and esp. J. Pardo Tomás, 'Le immagini delle piante americane nell' opera di Gonzalo Fernández de Oviedo (1478–1557)', in G. Olmi, L. Tongiorgi Tomasi and A. Zanca, eds, *Natura-Cultura: L'interpretazione del mondo fisico nei testi e nelle immagini* (Florence, 2000), pp. 163–88.

4 F. Lestringant, *L'Experience huguenote au nouveau monde (XVIᵉ siècle)* (Geneva, 1996), pp. 63–76. An Italian translation of the *Singularitez* by Giuseppe Horologgi published in Venice in 1561 did not reproduce the woodcuts of the French edition.

5 G. Olmi, *L'inventario del mondo: Catalogazione della natura e luoghi del sapere nella prima età moderna* (Bologna, 1992), p. 39.

6 The earliest European representation of American armadillos are to be found on maps like that of Diego Ribeiro from 1529, now in the Vatican Library; see W. George, *Animals and Maps* (London, 1969). If the artist of the armadillo added to a manuscript of Pietro Candido Decembrio's *De omnium animalium naturis atque*

formis (Cod. Urb. Lat. 276, Biblioteca Apostolica Vaticana, Rome) was a disciple or imitator of Raphael such as Giulio Romano or Giovanni da Udine, his rendering is one of the earliest illustrations of this creature; see D. Franchini *et al.*, *La Scienza a Corte: Collezionismo eclettico, natura e immagine a Mantova fra Rinascimento e Manierismo* (Rome, 1979), pp. 65–8. On the early iconography of the armadillo – a very popular creature in the European *Kunst- und Wunderkammern* – see also F. Egmond and P. Mason, 'Armadillos in Unlikely Places: Some Unpublished Sixteenth-Century Sources for New World *Rezeptionsgeschichte* in Northern Europe', *Ibero-Amerikanisches Archiv*, XX/ 1–2 (1994), pp. 3–52.

7   N. Dacos, 'Présents américains à la Renaissance: L'Assimilation de l'exotisme', *Gazette des Beaux-Arts*, LXXXIII (1969), pp. 57–64.

8   H. Honour, 'Science and Exoticism: The European Artist and the Non-European World before Johan Maurits', in E. van den Boogaart, ed., *Johan Maurits van Nassau-Siegen 1604–1679: A Humanist Prince in Europe and Brazil* (The Hague, 1979), p. 271.

9   W. B. Ashworth Jr, 'The Persistent Beast: Recurring Images in Early Zoological Illustration', in A. Ellenius, ed., *The Natural Sciences and the Arts* (Stockholm, 1985), p. 58.

10   H. Honour, ed., *L'Amérique vue par l'Europe*, exh. cat., Grand Palais, Paris (1976), p. 47.

11   H. E. van Gelder, 'Twee Braziliaanse schildpadden door Albert Eckhout', *Oud Holland*, LXXV (1960), pp. 5–29. The painting is now in the Mauritshuis, The Hague.

12   This woodcut was copied for the 1495 edition of the same work and, in reverse, for the first edition of Vespucci's letters to Soderini (Florence, 1505–6). It has been widely reproduced; see, for example, Honour, ed., *L'Amérique vue par l'Europe*, p. 7.

13   Sturtevant, 'First Visual Images', p. 420.

14   The Eckhout paintings are called 'the earliest full-length figure paintings of exotic people in European art' in R. Joppien, 'The Dutch Vision of Brazil: Johan Maurits and His Artists', in Van den Boogaart, ed., *Johan Maurits van Nassau-Siegen*, p. 302. On the alleged ethnographic realism of these paintings, see P. Mason, 'Portrayal and Betrayal: The Colonial Gaze in Seventeenth-Century Brazil', *Culture and History*, VI (1989), pp. 37–62.

15   M. Bloch, *The Historian's Craft*, trans. P. Putnam (New York, 195), p. 29.

16   'Origin [Ursprung], although an entirely historical category, has, nevertheless, nothing to do with genesis [Entstehung]' (W. Benjamin, *The Origin of German Tragic Drama*, trans. J. Osborne [London, 1977], p. 45). See the developments of this insight in G. Didi-Huberman, *Devant le temps: Histoire de l'art et anachronisme des images* (Paris, 2000), esp. pp. 82–3, 239ff.

17   J.-P. Digard, *L'Homme et les animaux domestiques: Anthropologie d'une passion* (Paris, 1990), p. 132. On the role of the turkey in the diets of sixteenth-century America and Europe, see A. Garrido Aranda, 'La revolución alimentaria del sigo XVI en América y Europa', in M. Gutiérrez Estévez, ed., *Sustentos, aflicciones y postrimerías de los Indios de América* (Madrid, 2000), p. 22.

18   L. L. Möller, 'Der Indianische Hahn in Europa', in M. Barasch, L. Freeman Sandler and P. Egan, eds, *Art the Ape of Nature: Studies in Honor of H. W. Janson* (New York, 1981), pp. 313–40; L. Plouvier, 'Introduction de la dinde en Europe', *Scientiarium Historia*, XXI/ 1 (1995), pp. 13–34.

19   Möller, 'Der Indianische Hahn', p. 313.

20   E. and D. Panofsky, 'The Iconography of the Galerie François Ier at

Fontainebleau', *Gazette des Beaux-Arts*, LII (1958), p. 165 n. 14.

21 E. Scheicher, *Das Brettspiel Kaiser Ferdinands I* (Vienna, 1986). Though the game would not have been out of place in the collection of Archduke Ferdinand II (1529–1595) in Schloß Ambras, Innsbruck, there is nothing in the inventories to support such an assumption.

22 *L'École de Fontainebleau*, exh. cat., Grand Palais (Paris, 1972), no. 284; M. de Jong and I. de Groot, *Ornamentenprenten in Het Rijksprentenkabinet I. 15de & 16de eeuw* (The Hague, 1988), no. 578.16.

23 Later examples are the turkey in the Loggie of Gregory XIII on the first floor of the Palazzo Vaticano, attributed to Mattys Bril and dating from around 1575, and the turkey depicted opposite a European cock and hen in the unusual pose of eating a bunch of grapes in the pergola in the Palazzo Rospigliosi Pallavicini, attributed to Paul Bril and dating from the early seventeenth century; see A. Negro, *Il giardino dipinto del Cardinale Borghese: Paolo Bril e Guido Reni nel Palazzo Rospigliosi Pallavicini* (Rome, 1996), pp. 45–6.

24 The artist of this woodcut is not Pierre Gourdelle but an otherwise unknown artist called Pierre Goudet; see the introduction by P. Glardon to his facsimile edition of Pierre Belon du Mans, *L'Histoire de la Nature des Oyseaux* (Geneva, 1997), pp. xxxix–xl.

25 C. Avery, *Giambologna: The Complete Sculpture* (London, 1987), p. 154. The German flask is illustrated in K.-H. Kohl, *Mythen der Neuen Welt* (Berlin, 1982), no. 4/73; see Möller, 'Der Indianische Hahn', fig. 8.

26 J. Szablowski *et al.*, *The Flemish Arrases of the Royal Castle in Cracow* (Warsaw, 1996), p. 263.

27 In addition to the examples listed by Möller, see the copper engraving of a 'Gallus cornutus' and 'Gallus Indicus' from the series *Avium vivae icones* by Adriaen Collaert (*Mythen der Neuen Welt*, no. 4/41), copied on a Dutch majolica panel of 54 birds, flowers and insects from *c.* 1620–40 (P. Biesboer, *Nederlandse majolica 1550–1650* [Haarlem, 1997], no. 174), and the series of birds by Hans Collaert and Marcus Geerarts (*Ornamentenprenten*, no. 70.1). In 1582, Allori added an American turkey to Andrea del Sarto's 1521 *Tribute to Caesar*; see C. Lazzaro, 'Animals as Cultural Signs: A Medici Menagerie in the Grotto at Castello', in C. Farago, ed., *Reframing the Renaissance* (New Haven, 1995), p. 223.

28 Identification as a llama in Kohl, ed., *Mythen der Neuen Welt*, no. 8/1 and Honour, ed., *L'Amérique vue par l'Europe*, p. 91. Contra: S. Poeschel, *Studien zur Ikonographie der Erdteile in der Kunst des 16.–18. Jahrhunderts* (Munich, 1985); A. Wendt, *Kannibalismus in Brasilien* (Frankfurt, 1989), p. 193 n. 2.

29 The rhinoceros also appears on an ink drawing by an anonymous Flemish artist around 1600 (illustrated in Honour, ed., *L'Amérique vue par l'Europe*, p. 93). The opossum-like creature in the background of the scene on the German plaque is a *su*; see Egmond and Mason, 'Armadillos', pp. 15–16.

30 'Here, more than elsewhere, the dichotomy between the central scene and the frame becomes visible' (*L'École de Fontainebleau*, no. 284).

31 Honour, 'Science and Exoticism', p. 289, pl. 144; P. Morel, *Les Grotesques: Les Figures de l'Imaginaire dans la Peinture Italienne de la fin de la Renaissance* (Paris, 1997), p. 70.

32 A post-conquest example can be found in the *Codex Florentino* (vol. 111, fol. 182r), which was painted on European paper in the second half of the sixteenth century; see S. Gruzinski, *Painting the Conquest: The Mexican Indians and the European Renaissance* (Paris, 1992), p. 196.

33 For post-conquest examples from the *Codex Florentino* (vol. 111, fol. 178r) and the *Codex Magliabechiano* (fol. 61r), see *ibid.*, pp. 197 and 62 respectively.

34   'Marvels of the East: A Study in the History of Monsters' is reprinted in R.
     Wittkower, *Allegory and the Migration of Symbols* (London, 1977), pp. 46–74; see
     J. B. Friedman, *The Monstrous Races in Medieval Art and Thought* (Cambridge,
     MA, 1981).

35   See C. Lecouteux, *Les Monstres dans la Littérature Allemande du Moyen Age*
     (Göppingen, 1982), vol. 11, pp. 20–26.

36   E. Magaña, 'Note on Ethnoanthropological Notions of the Guiana Indians',
     Anthropologica, XXIV (1982), pp. 215–33; P. Mason, *Deconstructing America:
     Representations of the Other* (London, 1990); *idem*, 'De l'articulation', *L'Homme*,
     XXX/114 (1990), pp. 27–49; *idem*, 'Half a Cow', *Semiotica*, LXXXV (1991),
     pp. 1–39; *idem*, 'Classical Ethnology and Its Influence on the European
     Perception of the Peoples of the New World', in W. Haase and M. Reinhold, eds,
     *The Classical Tradition and the Americas, vol. I, pt. 1. European Images of the
     Americas and the Classical Tradition* (Berlin and New York, 1994), pp. 135–72; D.
     White, *Myths of the Dog-Man* (Chicago, 1991); V. I. J. Flint, *The Imaginative
     Landscape of Christopher Columbus* (Princeton, 1992).

37   P. Mason, 'Seduction from Afar: Europe's Inner Indians', *Anthropos*, LXXXII
     (1987), p. 583.

38   Sturtevant, in 'First Visual Images', p. 419, comments: '… the first convincing
     European paintings of Indian physiognomy and body build of which I am aware
     are those by Albert Eckhout done in Brazil in 1641–43.'

39   L. Laurencich-Minelli, *Un 'giornale' del Cinquecento sulla scoperta dell'America:
     Il Manoscritto di Ferrara* (Milan, 1985), figs 30, 61.

40   J. M. Massing, 'Early European Images of America: The Ethnographic
     Approach', in J. A. Levenson, ed., *Circa 1492: Art in the Age of Exploration*, exh.
     cat. (New Haven, 1991), pp. 515–16.

41   *Ibid.*, no. 405; see also C. F. Feest, 'The Collecting of American Indian Artifacts
     in Europe, 1493–1750', in K. Ordahl Kupperman, *America in European
     Consciousness, 1493–1750* (Chapel Hill, 1995), p. 332; J. Rowlands, 'Prints and
     Drawings', in A. MacGregor, *Sir Hans Sloane: Collector, Scientist, Antiquary,
     Founding Father of the British Museum* (London, 1994), p. 257.

42   Massing, 'Early European Images', p. 516. There is no need to assume that this is
     the club which André Thevet brought back with him; see P. Mason, 'From
     Presentation to Representation: *Americana* in Europe', *Journal of the History of
     Collections*, VI (1994), p. 3.

43   Now in the Alte Pinothek, Munich. See Honour, 'Science and Exoticism',
     p. 290.

44   Honour, ed., *L'Amérique vue par l'Europe*, p. 10; Levenson, ed., *Circa 1492*,
     no. 32.

45   On coconut beakers, see R. Fritz, *Gefässe aus Kokosnuss in Mitteleuropa:
     1250–1800* (Mainz, 1983).

46   Massing, 'Early European Images', p. 516.

47   Sturtevant, 'First Visual Images', p. 426.

48   Massing, 'Early European Images', p. 518, takes these feathers to be a later
     addition. On the contamination of Mexico and Peru with Brazil in Montaigne's
     essay *Des Cannibales*, see F. Lestringant, *Le Huguenot et le Sauvage: L'Amérique et
     la controverse coloniale, en France, au temps des Guerres de Religion (1555–1589)*
     (Paris, 1990), p. 251.

49   See the examples in P. Mason, *Infelicities: Representations of the Exotic* (Baltimore,
     1998), pp. 18ff.

50   The fullest discussion of Harman and the Harman monument to date is
     contained in a paper by the late Michael Balfour, *Edmund Harman, Barber and*

Gentleman, which was published as Tolsey Paper no. 6 by the Tolsey Museum, Burford, in 1988. Harman appears (with and without beard) in two paintings by Hans Holbein; see B. Cohen, 'King Henry VIII and the Barber Surgeons: The Story of the Holbein Cartoon', *Annals of the Royal College of Surgeons of England*, XL (1967), pp. 179–94; *idem*, 'A Tale of Two Paintings', *Annals of the Royal College of Surgeons of England*, LXIV (1982), pp. 3–12.

51 W. C. Sturtevant, 'La Tupinambisation des indiens d'Amérique du Nord', in G. Thérien, ed., *Les Figures de l'Indien* (Montreal, 1988), pp. 293–303.

52 Sturtevant, 'First Visual Images', pp. 439–40.

53 S. Piggott, *Ruins in a Landscape* (Edinburgh, 1976), pp. 25–32. Piggott notes that the identification of the figures as Brazilian Indians was supported by Profs David Quinn and Virginia Rau. An identification of them as Indians, albeit North American ones, is accepted by A. Wells-Cole, *Art and Decoration in Elizabethan and Jacobean England: The Influence of Continental Prints, 1558–1625* (New Haven, 1997), p. 51.

54 Piggott, *Ruins*, p. 28.

55 S. Smiles, 'A Native American in Stone: The Simcoe Memorial in Exeter Cathedral', in M. Gidley, ed., *Representing Others: White Views of Indigenous Peoples* (Exeter, 1992), pp. 14–24.

56 E. Chirelstein, 'Lady Elizabeth Pope: The Heraldic Body', in L. Gent and N. Llewellyn, eds, *Renaissance Bodies. The Human Figure in English Culture, c. 1540–1660* (London, 1990), pp. 36–59.

57 Piggott, *Ruins*, p. 28.

58 *Ibid.*, p. 30. This native American spent one year in England and died on the return voyage to his native country.

59 Sturtevant, 'First Visual Images', p. 427, refers to 'superb Tupinamba figures on the Brazilian coast ... clearly based on first-hand information'.

60 *Ibid.*, p. 440.

61 Sturtevant, 'La Tupinambisation'.

62 On the cartouche with French proverb, see S. Schéle, *Cornelis Bos: A Study in the Origins of the Netherlands Grotesque* (Stockholm, 1965), p. 185. The identification of the sculptor's sources was first made by Wells-Cole; see *Art and Decoration*, pp. 15 (Serlio), 51 (Bos).

63 Schéle, *Cornelis Bos*, pp. 79–80.

64 The hypothetical biography of Bos by Schéle requires modification on a number of points in light of a more recent study based on archival sources: P. van der Coelen, 'Cornelis Bos – Where Did He Go? Some New Discoveries and Hypotheses about a Sixteenth-century Engraver and Publisher', *Simiolus*, XXIII (1995), pp. 119–46.

65 Sturtevant, 'La Tupinambisation', p. 296; *idem*, 'What Does the Plains Indian War Bonnet Communicate?', in D. Eban, E. Cohen and B. Danet, eds, *Art as a Means of Communication in Pre-Literate Societies* (Jerusalem, 1990), p. 359 n. 24. The feather crown in Copenhagen (inv. no. Ehc56) is illustrated in B. Dam-Mikkelsen and T. Lundbæk, eds, *Etnografiske genstande i Det kongelige danske Kunstkammer 1650–1800* (Copenhagen, 1980), p. 30, and (in colour) in B. Gundestrup, *Det kongelige danske Kunstkammer 1737*, vol. 11 (Copenhagen, 1991), p. 121.

66 On the figure of Quoniambec, see F. Lestringant, 'The Myth of the Indian Monarchy: An Aspect of the Controversy between Thevet and Léry (1575–1585)', in C. Feest, ed., *Indians and Europe: An Interdisciplinary Collection of Essays* (Aachen, 1987), pp. 37–60; *idem*, *L'Atelier du cosmographe ou l'image du monde à la Renaissance* (Paris, 1991), pp. 129–45.

67 Sturtevant, 'First Visual Images', p. 421; Massing, 'Early European Images', p. 516. According to Honour, 'Science and Exoticism', p. 277, this is the first representation of maize in European art. See also M. Dos Santos Lopes, 'Tradition und Imagination: "Kalikutische Leut" im Kontext alt-neuer Weltbeschreibungen des 16. Jahrhunderts', in D. Lombard and R. Ptak, eds, *Asia Maritima: Images et réalité: Bilder und Wirklichkeit 1200–1800* (Wiesbaden, 1994),
pp. 13–26.

68 Sturtevant, 'First Visual Images', p. 440.

69 Dacos, 'Présents américains'. On the importance of the discovery of the Domus Aurea, see N. Dacos, *La Découverte de la Domus Aurea et la formation des grotesques à la Renaissance* (London, 1969). An early example of the influence of the Domus Aurea can be seen in a set of ornamental prints by Nicoletta da Modena, who saw the building in 1507 and may have published the prints in the same year; see E. Miller, *16th-Century Italian Ornamental Prints in the Victoria and Albert Museum* (London, 1999), p. 76.

70 F. R. Sharpley, 'A Note on "The Three Philosophers" by Giorgione', *Art Quarterly*, XXII (1959), pp. 241–3. On the enigmatic iconography of this painting, see S. Settis, *Giorgione's Tempest: Interpreting the Hidden Subject*, trans. E. Bianchini (Cambridge, 1990).

71 To confine ourselves to examples from the collection in the Print Room in Amsterdam (the following numbers refer to the catalogue by M. de Jong and I. de Groot, *Ornamentenprenten*), we can note the presence of tropical fruit attached to poles or cords (2.1, Arend van Bolten; 60.9, Theodor de Bry; 72.2, Dirck Volckertsz. Coornhert; 74.1, Cornelis Floris), palmette head-dresses (12.7, Cornelis Bos) and palmette head-dresses in combination with feathered skirts (76.1, Cornelis Floris).

72 On Piero's paintings of the early history of humankind, see esp. E. Panofsky, *Studies in Iconology* (New York, 1962), pp. 33–67; S. Fermor, *Piero di Cosimo: Fiction, Invention and Fantasia* (London, 1993).

73 Mason, *Infelicities*, pp. 16–41.

74 Balfour, *Edmund Harman*, p. 14; Wells-Cole, *Art and Decoration*, pp. 51–2.

4 The Purloined Codex

1 M. Jansen, 'The Search for History in Mixtec Codices', *Ancient Mesoamerica*, I (1990), pp. 99–100.

2 O. Worm, *Museum Wormianum* (Amsterdam, 1655), p. 383. Compare the woodcuts in L. Legati, *Museo Cospiano* (1677) taken from the *Codex Cospi*; they are reproduced in K.-H. Kohl, ed., *Mythen der Neuen Welt* (Berlin, 1982), illus. 145, 147.

3 As suggested by P. Burke, 'America and the Rewriting of World History', in K. Ordahl Kupperman, ed., *America in European Consciousness, 1493–1750* (Chapel Hill, 1995), pp. 39–40; see also P. Burke, *A Social History of Knowledge from Gutenberg to Diderot* (Cambridge, 2000), pp. 70, 194.

4 R. Wittkower, *Allegory and the Migration of Symbols* (London, 1977), pp. 15–44.

5 The most detailed biography of Thevet is F. Lestringant, *André Thevet: Cosmographe des derniers Valois* (Geneva, 1991).

6 Venice, 1561; London, 1568. For a full bibliography of the various editions of Thevet's writings, see *ibid.*, pp. 369ff.

7 The dates of Thevet's ex libris are not always reliable; sometimes, they even antedate the publication date of the work in which they appear; see *ibid.*,

pp. 39–40.

8 B. Keen, *The Aztec Image in Western Thought* (New Brunswick, 1971), p. 207.

9 On the circulation of woodcuts based on the *Codex Mendoza*, see *ibid.* and H. B. Nicholson, 'The History of the Codex Mendoza', in F. F. Berdan and P. R. Anawalt, eds, *The Codex Mendoza* (Berkeley, 1992), vol. 1, pp. 1–11.

10 Lestringant, *André Thevet*, p. 384; C. Duverger, *L'Origine des Aztèques* (Paris, 1983), pp. 35–6.

11 Keen, *The Aztec Image*, pp. 151–5.

12 Twelve chapters from this work, six on European explorers and six on native American 'chiefs', have been translated into English and annotated; see R. Schlesinger, ed., *Selections from André Thevet's Les vrais pourtraits et vies des hommes illustres*, trans. E. Benson (Urbana, 1993).

13 The British alchemist John Dee also included genealogies of 'Altabalipa' and of the kings of Mexico in a manuscript on the kings of Spain and England; see W. H. Sherman, *John Dee: The Politics of Reading and Writing in the English Renaissance* (Amherst, 1995), p. 10 n. 29.

14 André Theuet, *Les Vrais Pourtraits* (Paris, 1584), fols 623–63.

15 W. C. Sturtevant, 'First Visual Images of Native America', in F. Chiappelli, ed., *First Images of America* (Berkeley, 1976), vol. 1, p. 438; *idem*, 'Indian America: First Visual Impressions in Europe', in S. A. Bedini, ed., *The Christopher Columbus Encyclopedia* (New York, 1991), p. 340.

16 R. Joppien, 'Etude de quelques portraits ethnologiques dans l'oeuvre d'André Thevet', *Gazette des Beaux-Arts* (1978), pp. 125–36.

17 C. F. Feest, 'Vienna's Mexican Treasures: Aztec, Mixtec, and Tarascan Works from 16th Century Austrian Collections', *Archiv für Völkerkunde*, XLIV (1990), pp. 13–14; F. Anders and P. Kann, *Die Schätze des Montezuma: Utopie und Wirklichkeit* (Vienna, 1996), p. 10.

18 Thevet commissioned various Flemish artists to execute the engravings; see Lestringant, *André Thevet*, p. 377.

19 P. R. Anawalt, 'A Comparative Analysis of the Costumes and Accoutrements of the Codex Mendoza', in Berdan and Anawalt, eds, *The Codex Mendoza*, vol. 1, p. 122.

20 On the difficulties encountered by the artist in trying to adopt one-point perspective, see K. S. Howe, 'The Relationship of Indigenous and European Styles in the *Codex Mendoza*: An Analysis of Pictorial Style', in Berdan and Anawalt, eds, *The Codex Mendoza*, pp. 29–30.

21 Joppien, 'Etude', p. 130.

22 F. Lestringant, *Le Huguenot et le Sauvage: L'Amérique et la controverse coloniale, en France, au temps des Guerres de Religion (1555–1589)* (Paris, 1990), p. 191. At a later period, Inca nobles appear with solar medallions on their chests to emphasize their privileged status in Christian society; see T. B. Cummins, 'We Are the Other: Peruvian Portraits of Colonial *Kurakakuna*', in K. J. Andrien and R. Adorno, eds, *Transatlantic Encounters: Europeans and Andeans in the Sixteenth Century* (Berkeley, 1991), pp. 203–31.

23 F. Lestringant, ed., *Le Brésil d'André Thevet: Les Singularités de la France Antarctique (1557)* (Paris, 1997), p. 286; C. F. Feest, 'Jacques Le Moyne Minus Four', *European Review of Native American Studies*, I/1 (1988), p. 35.

24 F. Lestringant, 'The Myth of the Indian Monarchy: An Aspect of the Controversy between Thevet and Léry (1575–1585)', in C. Feest, ed., *Indians and Europe: An Interdisciplinary Collection of Essays* (Aachen, 1987), pp. 39ff. For Ludovico Buti's Herculean rendering of Mexican warriors, see chap. 6.

25 F. Egmond and P. Mason, *The Mammoth and the Mouse: Microhistory and*

Morphology (Baltimore, 1997), pp. 168ff.

26 Pliny, *Historia Naturalis*, xxv, 2; see A. Schnapper, *Le Géant, La Licorne, La Tulipe: Collections françaises au XVIIe siècle* (Paris, 1988), pp. 125–6.

27 L. Cheles, *Lo studiolo di Urbino: Iconografia di un microcosmo principesco* (Modena, 1991), pp. 37–54, 97–9.

28 Lestringant, *André Thevet*, p. 279. François de Belleforest, like Thevet the author of a vernacular *Cosmographie*, also had plans for a *Catalogue des hommes illustres* in the 1570s; see M. Simonin, *Vivre de sa plume au XVIe siècle, ou la carrière de François de Belleforest* (Geneva, 1992), p. 214.

29 Lestringant, 'The Myth', p. 44.

30 R. Trexler, *Church and Community 1200–1600* (Rome, 1987), pp. 469–92.

31 Sturtevant, 'First Visual Images', pp. 437–8 and n. 45; see Feest, 'Jacques Le Moyne', pp. 33–8.

32 The name 'Peru' first appears in published costume books in Jost Amman's *Habitus praecipuorum populorum* (1577), but it is used there as a synonym for 'Brazil'; see N. Pellegrin, 'Vêtements de peau(x) et de plumes: La Nudité des indiens et la diversité du monde au XVIe siècle', in J. Céard and J.-C. Margolin, eds, *Voyager à la Renaissance: Actes du colloque de Tours 1983* (Paris, 1987), p. 520 n. 37.

33 Lestringant, *Le Huguenot*, p. 251.

34 *Ibid.*, p. 144.

35 P. Mason, 'From Presentation to Representation: *Americana* in Europe', *Journal of the History of Collections* VI/1 (1994), pp. 1–20.

36 C. F. Feest, 'The Collecting of American Indian Artifacts in Europe, 1493–1750', in K. Ordahl Kupperman, ed., *America in European Consciousness, 1493–1750* (Chapel Hill, 1995), p. 335.

37 M. Gianoncelli, *L'Antico Museo di Paolo Giovio in Borgovico* (Como, 1977), pp. 39–40; T. C. P. Zimmermann, *Paolo Giovio* (Princeton, 1995), pp. 159–63; G. Olmi, *L'inventario del mondo: Catalogazione della natura e luoghi del sapere nella prima età moderna* (Bologna, 1992), p. 258 n. 11. Barbarossa was represented on fol. 648 of Thevet's *Les Vrais Pourtraits*.

38 E. Scheicher, 'The Collection of Archduke Ferdinand II at Schloß Ambras: Its Purpose, Composition and Evolution', in O. Impey and A. MacGregor, eds, *The Origins of Museums* (Oxford, 1985), pp. 29–38.

39 C. Ginzburg, 'Montaigne, Cannibals and Grottoes', *History and Anthropology*, VI/2–3 (1993), p. 140.

40 Sturtevant, 'First Visual Images', p. 438 n. 46.

41 F. Egmond and P. Mason, 'Armadillos in Unlikely Places: Some Unpublished Sixteenth-Century Sources for New World *Rezeptionsgeschichte* in Northern Europe', *Ibero-Amerikanisches Archiv*, XX/1–2 (1994), p. 19.

42 On Dürer, see E. Panofsky, *The Life and Art of Albrecht Dürer* (Princeton, 1971), p. 36; Levenson, *Circa 1492*, no. 110. On Weiditz's drawings of native Americans, see J. M. Massing, 'Early European Images of America: The Ethnographic Approach', in *ibid.*, pp. 517–18. On costume books, see Pellegrin, 'Vêtements'; D. Defert, 'Les Collections iconographiques du XVIe siècle', in Céard and Margolin, eds, *Voyager à la Renaissance,* pp. 531–43.

43 Feest, 'Jacques Le Moyne'.

44 Lestringant, *André Thevet*, pp. 301–41.

45 Keen, *The Aztec Image*, pp. 190, 261–2; C. de Pauw, *Recherches philosophiques sur les Américains* (Berlin, 1774), vol. 11, p. 152.

46 C. Acidini Luchinat, ed., *Trésors des Médicis* (Paris, 1997), p. 165.

47 Lestringant, *André Thevet*, pp. 286–9.

48 F. Lestringant, 'The Euhemerist Tradition and the European Perception and Description of the American Indians', in W. Haase and M. Reinhold, eds, *The Classical Tradition and the Americas, vol. I, pt. 1. European Images of the Americas and the Classical Tradition* (Berlin and New York, 1994), p. 181; see *idem, Le Cannibale: Grandeur et décadence* (Paris, 1994), p. 188.

49 J. Friedman, *Miracles and the Pulp Press during the English Revolution: The Battle of the Frogs and Fairford's Flies* (London, 1993), p. 50.

50 *Ibid.*, p. 273 n. 1.

51 There is a precedent for the coincidence of a spate of publications on monstrous births with a period of political and religious turbulence in the 1560s; understandably, the powers that be were intent on controlling or neutralizing anything that augured a change in the status quo. See D. Cressy, *Travesties and Transgressions in Tudor and Stuart England* (Oxford, 2000), pp. 9–28. For other monstrous births in the sixteenth and seventeenth centuries, see D. Wilson, *Signs and Portents: Monstrous Births from the Middle Ages to the Enlightenment* (London, 1993), pp. 72–100.

52 The title page of the pamphlet is reproduced in Friedman, *Miracles*, p. 224, but I have not been able to trace any reference to it in the body of his text.

53 R. Blanchard, 'Sur quelques géants américains', *Journal de la Société des Américanistes de Paris*, VI (1909), pp. 45–62.

54 H. Hofmann, '*Adveniat tandem Typhis qui detegat orbes*: Columbus in Neo-Latin Epic Poetry (15th–18th centuries)', in Haase and Reinhold, eds, *The Classical Tradition*, p. 650.

55 T. Gisbert, *Iconografía y Mitos Indígenas en el Arte* (La Paz, 1980), pp. 149ff.

56 Colonial painting reveals a similar confusion of Atahualpa and Tupac Amaru in representations of their deaths. While Atahualpa was executed by *garrote vil* and Tupac Amaru was decapitated, a number of representations of the death of the former portray him being decapitated; see M. López-Baralt, 'The *Yana K'uychi* or Black Rainbow in Atawallpa's Elegy: A Look at the Andean Metaphor of Liminality in a Cultural Context', in E. Magaña and P. Mason, eds, *Myth and Imaginary in the New World* (Amsterdam, 1986), pp. 261–303; G. Weiss, 'Elements of Inkarrí East of the Andes', in *ibid.*, pp. 305–20.

57 S. L. Catlin, 'Political Iconography in the Diego Rivera Frescoes at Cuernavaca, Mexico', in H. A. Millon and L. Nochlin, *Art and Architecture in the Service of Politics* (Cambridge, 1978), pp. 194–215.

58 Illustrated in Levenson, ed., *Circa 1492*, no. 385. Though the Eagle Knight is documented in five Aztec pictorial sources, it is nowhere to be found in the *Codex Mendoza*; see Anawalt, 'A Comparative Analysis', p. 122.

59 B. Braun, *Pre-Columbian Art and the Post-Columbian World: Ancient American Sources of Modern Art* (New York, 1993), pp. 208–9.

60 Keen, *The Aztec Image*, p. 530.

61 Braun, *Pre-Columbian Art*, p. 234.

62 G. Brett, 'Unofficial versions', in S. Hiller, ed., *The Myth of Primitivism: Perspectives on Art* (London, 1991), p. 127.

63 Remarkably, Rivera is nowhere mentioned in R. Goldwater, *Primitivism in Modern Art* (Cambridge, 1986), the revised and enlarged edition of his classic *Primitivism in Modern Painting* (1938). Rivera is only touched upon briefly, in a discussion of the relationship between Surrealism and anthropology, in the more recent treatment by C. Rhodes, *Primitivism and Modern Art* (London, 1994), p. 81.

64 S. Gruzinski, *Painting the Conquest: The Mexican Indians and the European Renaissance* (Paris, 1992), p. 189.

65 The information in this paragraph is drawn mainly from the researches of Francesco Solinas, 'Il primo erbario azteco e la copia romana di Cassiano dal Pozzo', in *Il Museo Cartaceo di Casiano dal Pozzo: Cassiano naturalista, Quaderni Puteani I* (Milan, 1989), pp. 77–83; 'Other Sources of Drawings in the Paper Museum', in *The Paper Museum of Cassiano dal Pozzo, Quaderni Puteani IV* (Milan, 1993), pp. 225–42.

66 *Quaderni Puteani IV*, pp. 36–7. On this artist's prolific output, see F. Solinas, *L'Uccelliera: Un libro di arte e di scienza nella Roma dei primi Lincei* (Florence, 2000), pp. 51ff.

67 On the role of the *Tesoro Messicano* within the activities of the Accademia dei Lincei, see A. Nicoló, 'Il carteggio puteano: ricerche e aggiornamenti', in F. Solinas, ed., *Cassiano dal Pozzo: Atti del Seminario Internazionale di Studi* (Rome, 1987), p. 16; G. Olmi, *L'inventario del mondo: Catalogazione della natura e luoghi del sapere nella prima età moderna* (Bologna, 1992), pp. 315–79. On Cassiano dal Pozzo's contacts with other collectors of his time, see D. L. Sparti, *Le collezioni dal Pozzo: Storia di una famiglia e del suo museo nella Roma seicentesca* (Modern Modena, 1992), pp. 83–91.

68 Braun, *Pre-Columbian Art*, pp. 225–6.

5 Images and Objects

1 P. Mason, 'From Presentation to Representation: *Americana* in Europe', *Journal of the History of Collections*, VI/1 (1994), p. 3. On the role of Thevet and other French travellers in the Middle East in the middle of the sixteenth century, see F. Tingueley, *L'Ecriture du levant à la Renaissance* (Geneva, 2000).

2 On the Medici collections, see C. Acidini Luchinat, ed., *Trésors des Médicis* (Paris, 1997).

3 On the presence of other Mexican codices in Italian collections, see A. A. Shelton, 'Cabinets of Transgression: Renaissance Collections and the Incorporation of the New World', in J. Elsner and R. Cardinal, eds, *The Cultures of Collecting* (London, 1994), p. 200.

4 D. Heikamp, 'Mexico und die Medici-Herzöge', in K.-H. Kohl, ed., *Mythen der Neuen Welt* (Berlin, 1982), pp. 126–46; see H. Honour, 'Science and Exoticism: The European Artist and the Non-European World before Johan Maurits', in E. van den Boogaart, ed., *Johan Maurits van Nassau-Siegen 1604–1679: A Humanist Prince in Europe and Brazil* (The Hague, 1979), pp. 286–7.

5 K. Pomian, *Collectionneurs, amateurs et curieux: Paris, Venise: XVIᵉ–XVIIIᵉ siècle* (Paris, 1987), p. 98.

6 The first illustrated edition, with figures by Bolognino Zaltieri, is that of 1571. Cartari's works include an abridgement of Paolo Giovio (*Il compendio dell'istoria di M. Paolo Giovio* [1562]).

7 The dependence of the images in Pignoria's appendix on this codex was established by J. Seznec, 'Un essai de mythologie comparée au début du XVIIᵉ siècle', *Mélanges d'histoire et d'archéologie* (1931), pp. 268–81. On the importance of Mexican codices, in particular *Codex Vaticanus A*, in sixteenth-century Italian repositories, see E. Quiñones Keber, 'Collecting Cultures: A Mexican Manuscript in the Vatican Library', in C. Farago, ed., *Reframing the Renaissance: Visual Culture in Europe and Latin America 1450–1650* (New Haven, 1995), pp. 228–42.

8 For information on the trajectory of this codex, I am indebted to F. Anders and M.E.R.G.N. Jansen, *Religión, Costumbres e Historia de los Antiguos Mexicanos: Libro explicativo del llamado Códice Vaticano A* (Mexico City, 1995).

9   S. MacCormack, 'Limits of Understanding: Perceptions of Graeco-Roman and
    Amerindian Paganism in Early Modern Europe', in K. Ordahl Kupperman, ed.,
    America in European Consciousness, 1493–1750 (Chapel Hill, 1995), p. 93.

10 For a survey that includes artists from both the Northern and the Southern
    Netherlands, see *Fiamminghi a Roma 1508–1608: Artistes des Pays-Bas et de la
    principauté de Liège à Rome à la Renaissance*, exh. cat., Palais des Beaux-Arts,
    Brussels (1995). On Winghe, see G. J. Hoogewerff, 'Philips van Winghe',
    Mededelingen van het Nederlandsch Historisch Instituut te Rome, VII (1927),
    pp. 59–82; G. Denhaene, 'Un témoignage de l'intérêt des humanistes flamands
    pour les gravures italiennes: Une lettre de Philippe van Winghe à Abraham
    Ortelius', *Bulletin de l'institut historique belge de Rome*, LXII (1992), pp. 69–137; C.
    Schuddeboom, 'Philips van Winghe (1560–1592) en het ontstaan van de
    christelijke archeologie', dissertation, Leiden, 1996.

11 D. Robertson, 'Mexican Indian Art and the Atlantic Filter: Sixteenth to
    Eighteenth Centuries', in F. Chiappelli, ed., *First Images of America* (Berkeley,
    1976), vol. 1, p. 490.

12 To the right of Quetzalcoatl, Winghe's annotation refers by name to 'F. Petrus a
    Rios Hispanus ordinis Praedicatorum'.

13 L. Seelig, 'The Munich *Kunstkammer*', in O. Impey and A. MacGregor, eds, *The
    Origins of Museums* (Oxford, 1985), p. 85.

14 D. Heikamp and F. Anders, 'Mexikanische Altertümer aus süddeutschen
    Kunstkammern', *Pantheon*, XXVIII (1970), p. 209. An edition of the 1598 Munich
    inventory is in preparation.

15 The correct identification of these two figures was made by C. Feest, '*Zemes
    Idolum Diabolicum*: Surprise and Success in Ethnographic Kunstkammer
    Research', *Archiv für Völkerkunde*, XL (1986), pp. 190–91. Feest's article
    supersedes the discussion of the same images in D. Heikamp, 'American Objects
    in Italian Collections of the Renaissance and Baroque: A Survey', in Chiappelli,
    ed., *First Images of America*, vol. 1, pp. 464–7.

16 Seznec, 'Un essai', p. 280.

17 For a survey of the role of artists, travellers and scientists in the discovery of
    Egypt, see F. Beaucour, Y. Laissus and C. Orgogozo, *The Discovery of Egypt*
    (Paris, 1990).

18 C. Farago, '"Vision Itself Has Its History": "Race", Nation, and Renaissance Art
    History', in Farago, ed., *Reframing the Renaissance*, p. 82.

19 This figure has been identified as the Aztec goddess Chalchiuhtlicue ('jade
    skirt'), associated with spring water, lakes and rivers; see C. MacLeod, *Ancient
    Mexico in the British Museum* (London, 1994), p. 73. The best discussion of the
    frontispiece to date is H. von Kügelgen Kropfinger, 'El frontispicio de François
    Gérard para la obra de viaje de Humboldt y Bonpland', *Jahrbuch für Geschichte
    von Staat, Wirtschaft und Gesellschaft Lateinamerikas*, XX (1983), pp. 575–616.

20 See F. Egmond and P. Mason, 'A Horse called Belisarius', *History Workshop*, XLVII
    (1999), pp. 240–51.

21 M. Jacobs, *The Painted Voyage: Art, Travel and Exploration 1564–1875* (London,
    1995), p. 132.

22 For the portraits, see H. Nelken, *Alexander von Humboldt: Bildnisse und Künstler:
    Eine dokumentierte Ikonographie* (Berlin, 1980). For Gérard's correspondence
    with Humboldt and other prominent figures and artists, see the letters edited by
    his nephew Henri Gérard in *Correspondance de François Gérard* (Paris, 1867), pp.
    202ff.

23 See Roger's steel engraving in Nelken, *Alexander von Humboldt*, p. 34.

24 Honour refers to 'un prince indien vaincu' (*L'Amérique vue par l'Europe*, exh.

cat., Grand Palais, Paris [1976], p. 234). M. Dettelbach, 'Humboldtian Science', in N. Jardine, J. A. Secord and E. C. Spary, eds, *Cultures of Natural History* (Cambridge, 1996), p. 302, also calls the figure a 'fallen Aztec prince', but in his 'Global Physics and Aesthetic Empire: Humboldt's Physical Portrait of the Tropics', in D. P. Miller and P. H. Reill, eds, *Visions of Empire: Voyages, Botany, and Representations of Nature* (Cambridge, 1996), p. 289, he refers to the 'fallen priestess'. A. Pagden, *European Encounters with the New World* (New Haven, 1993), p. 9, more circumspectly calls the figure a 'fallen Aztec'.

25 All of these identifications are made by H. von Kügelgen Kropfinger. in 'El frontispicio'.

26 K. E. Manthorne, *Tropical Renaissance: North American Artists Exploring Latin America 1839–1879* (Washington, DC, 1989), p. 91.

27 W. J. Rushing, *Native American Art and the New York Avant-Garde* (Austin, 1995).

28 J. Rabasa, 'Pre-Columbian Pasts and Indian Presents in Mexican History', *Dispositio/n*, XIX/46 (1994), p. 246.

29 It is instructive to contrast Humboldt's practice at this point with that of the colonial artist Augustus Earle (1793–1838), whose New Zealand paintings depict indigenous peoples as the occupiers of their own land; see N. Thomas, *Possessions: Indigenous Art/Colonial Culture* (London, 1999), pp. 54ff. The closest parallel to Humboldt's depopulation of the landscape in New Zealand would be the work of Colin McCahon (1919–1987); see *ibid.*, pp. 20ff. For useful comparisons between nineteenth-century depictions of Australian and American landscapes, see *New Worlds from Old: 19th Century Australian and American Landscapes*, exh. cat., National Gallery of Australia, Canberra (1998).

30 T. Webb, '"City of the Soul": English Romantic Travellers in Rome', in M. Liversidge and C. Edwards, eds, *Imagining Rome: British Artists and Rome in the Nineteenth Century* (London, 1996), p. 24.

31 J. Fabian, *Time and the Other: How Anthropology Makes Its Object* (New York, 1983).

32 On the relationship between the work of natural scientists and their physical bodies, see C. Lawrence and S. Shapin, eds, *Science Incarnate: Historical Embodiments of Natural Knowledge* (Chicago, 1998).

33 I. Jenkins and K. Sloan, eds, *Vases and Volcanoes: Sir William Hamilton and His Collection*, exh. cat., British Museum, London (1996).

34 W. Beckford, *Vathek and Other Stories*, ed. M. Jack (London, 1995), p. 24. Though Beckford wrote *The Long Story* in 1777 at the age of seventeen, its first English publication, as *The Vision*, occurred in 1930.

35 See Manthorne, *Tropical Renaissance*; P. Diener, 'Humboldt und die Kunst', in *Alexander von Humboldt: Netzwerke des Wissens*, exh. cat., Haus der Kulturen der Welt, Berlin (1999), pp. 137–53; *Explorar el Edén: Paisaje americano del siglo XIX*, exh. cat., Museo Thyssen-Bornemisza, Madrid (2000); R. D. Bedell, *The Anatomy of Nature: Geology and American Landscape Painting, 1825–1875* (Princeton, 2001).

Photographic Acknowledgements

The author and publisher wish to express their thanks to the following sources of illustrative material and/or permission to reproduce it:

Archivo de la Nación, Buenos Aires: 6, 16; Art Institute of Chicago ((William McCallin McKee Memorial Collection, 1112) - photos courtesy of the Art Institute of Chicago): 29 (folio 52 verso), 30 (folio 53 recto), 31 (folio 54 recto), 32 (folio 55 recto); Association pour la conservation et la reproduction photographique de la presse: 2; Biblioteca Apostolica Vaticana, Rome (Codex Vaticanus mess. 1): 65; Biblioteca Nacional de Chile: 35; Biblioteka Jagiellonska, Kraków: 40 (folio 59), 41 (folio 60), 42 (folio 35), 43 (folio 36); The Bodleian Library, University of Oxford ((Ms. Laud Misc. 678) - photos © The Bodleian Library)): 64, 66; The Bodleian Library, University of Oxford (Ms. Arch. Seld.A.1) - photos © The Bodleian Library: 71 (fol 2r), 78 (fol 62r), 79 (fol 15v), 82 (fol 65r), 87 (fol 60r); The British Library, London: 22 (Add. MS. 23920.11b), 23 (Add. MS. 23920.16), 24 (Add. MS. 23920.17), 25 (Add MS. 23920.18(b)), 26 (Add. MS. 23920.18), 27 (Add. MS. 23920.14a), 28 (Add. MS. 23920.13); Photos © 1996 The Detroit Institute of Arts/Dirk Bakker: 86, 88; Frans Hals Museum, Haarlem (photo Rijksdienst Beeldende Kunst): 70; Friends of Burford Church: 68; Koninklijke Bibliotheek, The Hague (MS 78 E 54, folio 39 verso): 37; Koninklijk Museum voor de Tropen, Amsterdam (photo Fotobureau): 15; Photo © Kunsthistorisch Instituut Amsterdam: 84; Lambeth Palace Library, London (Lambeth Palace Papers (No. 6, MS 954, item 27)): 44, 46, 48, 49, 51, 54, 55; Liverpool Free Public Library (M 12014, p. 6 (photo City of Liverpool Museums)): 63; Metropolitan Museum of Art, New York (Rogers Fund (Photo Metropolitan Museum of Art Photograph Services)): 62; Musée de l'Homme, Paris: 8, 9, 10, 11, 12, 13; Museo Artequín, Santiago, Chile: 4; Museum voor Volkenkunde, Rotterdam: 7; Museum Plantin-Moretus/Stedelijk Prentenkabinet, Antwerp: 17 (Cat. MPM 3806), 18 (Cat. III/C.147-150); The Newberry Library, Chicago: 14; The Pierpont Morgan Library, New York (MA 3900 (Peck Bequest) - photos Morgan Library): 38 (f. 88), 39 (f. 111); Rijksmuseum Amsterdam (photo © Rijksmuseum-Stichting Amsterdam): 59 (inv. no. RP-P-OB-67295); Staatliche Museen zu Berlin-Preussischer Kulturbesitz (Kupferstichkabinett)/ Jörg P. Anders: 61; Universidad de Chile: 3; Universiteits-bibliotheek Amsterdam: 19, 20, 21, 45, 47, 50, 52, 53, 56, 57, 67, 83, 97; courtesy of the artist: 33, 34, 36.

Index

Numerals in *italics* refer to illustrations

Achille I of Aruacania *see* Laviarde, Achille

Afonso de Albuquerque 9

Alakaluf, Fuegian canoe people *2*, 24-6

Albrecht V, Duke of Bavaria 101, 137

Aldrovandi, Ulisse 12, *119*, 122

Amulio, Cardinal Marco Antonio 132, *133*, 134

Amyot, Jacques 122

Atahualpa ('Atabalipa'), king of Peru *80*, 106, 112-3, 118, 120, 122, 123, 125, 129

Badiano, Juan 129

Balfour, Michael 94

Banks, Sir Joseph 42

Barbarossa (Khayr ad-Din) 120

Barberini, Cardinal Antonio 129

Bartolozzi, Francisco 43

Beckford, William 146

Belon, Pierre *60*, 83

Benedit, Luis Fernando 51

Benn, Tony 91

Berlin, Society for Anthropology, Ethnography and Prehistory 24

Bernini, Gianlorenzo 12

Bloch, Marc 82

Boas, Franz 28

Bolívar, Simón 144

Bonaparte, Prince Roland 17, 25, 35

Bonpland, Aimé 145

Bos, Cornelis *69*, 95-6, 97, 98, 99, 100

Boyvin, René *59*

Breslau Zoo 28

Breton, Richard 120

Breu, Jörg, Elder and Younger 83

Bridges, Lucas 22, 51

Bridges, Thomas 23

Bruijn, Abraham de 120

Brussels
    Musée Castan 21, 26, 30
    Musée du Nord 21, 29, 30
    Société d'Anthropologie de Bruxelles 28, 29-30

Buchan, Alexander 42-3, *22-4*

Burford, Oxfordshire, church of St John the Baptist, Harman monument at *68*, 91-100

Burgkmair, Hans 55, 89, 90, 91, 96

Buti, Ludovico 86, 131

Button, Jemmy (Orurdelicone) 23, *35*, 51

Calafate, José Luis *6*, *16*, 28

Candidius, George 77

Cartari, Vincenzo *90-96*, 132

Caso, Alfonso 126

Castello, Villa Medici 83

Catlin, George 45

Charles I, King of England and Scotland 123

Charles II, King of England and Scotland 125

Chimborazo, Mount 144, 146, 147

Church, Frederic 146

Church, John 91

Clavigero, Francisco Javier 102

Clement VII, Pope 101

Clüver, Philipp *83*

Codexes
    Badianus 129, 130
    Borbonicus 130
    Borgia 87, *65*
    Fejérvàry-Mayer 63, 86
    Florentino 125, 132
    Laud 64, 66, 86, 87
    Magliabechiana 132
    Mendoza 71, 78, 79, 82, 102-20, 121,

122, 125-8, *87*, 129, 140
Telleriano-Remensis 132, 133
Vaticanus 3738 (Vaticanus A) 132,
   133, 134, 135, 136, 137, 140, 143
Vindobonensis 132, 137
Coecke van Aalst, Pieter 84
Coenen, Adriaen *37*, 55, 56
Collaert, Adriaen *18*, 38
Collins, Wilkie 19, 78-9
Colonna, Michelangelo 119
Columbus, Christopher 21, 81, 88
Compton, Henry, Bishop of London 74
Cook, Captain James 23, 42, 43
Copenhagen, Ethnographic Museum 96
Cordes, Simon de 39
Cortavila y Sanabria, Diego 129
Cortes, Hernando 118
Cospi, Marchese Ferdinando 119
Cowley, Abraham 124
Cromwell, Oliver 91
Cromwell, Thomas 91
Cruz, Juan de la 129
Cuernavaca, Mexico, Cortés Palace 125
Cunningham, R. A. 25
Curtis, Edward 14

Dacos, Nicole 97
Darwin, Charles 16, 23, 51
De Bry, Theodor 39, 121
De Pauw, Cornelis 22, 122
De Rode, abbé 76, 77
De Sade, Donatien-Alphonse-François,
   Marquis 78
Degas, Edgar 47
Delacroix, Eugène 45
Delaune, Etienne *61*, 84, 85
Després, François 120
Didi-Huberman, Georges 15
Dittborn, Eugenio *33, 34*, 50
Doesborch, Jan van 96
Drake, Sir Francis 56
Drake Manuscript *see the Histoire
   naturelle des Indes*
Du Halde, Jean-Baptiste 77
Dürer, Albrecht 10, 13, 55, 82, 85, 89, 90,
   120

Eckhout, Albert 10, *40, 41*, 56, 71, 81
Ecluse, Charles de l' 81
Elisabeth of Valois, consort of Philip II
   of Spain 137
Ellis, William 79

Exeter Cathedral, Simcoe memorial at 93

Faber, Johann 129-30
Fabian, Johannes 145
Fabri de Peiresc, Nicolas-Claude 132
Federico II da Montefeltro, Duke of
   Urbino 116
Ferdinand I, Emperor 82
Ferdinand II, Archduke 120
Fergus, King of Scotland 112
Fernandes, Vasco 90
Fernández de Oviedo, Gonzalo 105
Ferroverde, Filippo 132
Fitz-Roy, Captain Robert 22, *35*
Flaubert, Gustave 47, 121
Flaxman, John 93
Florence, Uffizzi armoury 86, 131
Fontainebleau, School of 82, 83, 84, 96
Forster, Johann Reinhold 23
Fries, Lorenz 81
Frobisher, Martin 55
Fuegians, people of Terra del Fuego 2,
   6, *8-14*, 10-11, 16, *16*, 20, 22-54, *22-
   32, 35-6*
Fueguino, José *16*

Gérard, François *97*, 142, 144, 147
Gesner, Conrad 83
Giambologna (Jean de Bologne) 83
Ginzberg, Carlo 120
Giorgione (Giorgio da Castelfranco) 97
Giovanni da Udine 9
Giovio, Paulo 105, 116, 120
Giuliano di Domenico Dati 81
Godwin, Francis 72
Goethe, Johann Wolfgang von 144
Goudet, Pierre *60*
Gusinde, Martin 28, *53*, 54

Hagenbeck, Carl Jr 19-20, 24, 25
Hakluyt, Richard 16, 104
Halley, Edmund 75-6
Hamburg, Tierpark 20
Hamilton, Sir William 146
Harman, Edward, and his monument
   68, 91-100
Hawkins, William 94
Heemskerck, Maarten van 10
Henri II, King of France 116
Henry VIII, King of England 91, 94
Herwarth, Hans Georg 137
Histoire naturelle des Indes (Drake

Manuscript) *38-9*, 56, 80
Hodges, William 142
Holanda, Francisco de 10
Houzé, E. 29-30
Hovelacque 45
Humboldt, Alexander von 16, 142-7
Huyghen van Linschoten, Jan 70

Ickford, Buckinghamshire, church at 99-
    100
Innes, Revd Alexander 76-7
Isabella, Queen of Castile, consort of
    Ferdinand, King of Aragon 21

Jacques, V. 30
Jansen, Maarten 101
Johnson, Samuel 77
Joppien, Rüdiger 106-7, 112-14, 128

Kahlo, Frida 128
Kels, Hans the Elder 82
Khayr ad-Din (Barbarossa) 120
Khoikhoi people (Cape of Good Hope)
    56
Kircher, Athanasius 105
Krakow, Wawel Castle 84
Kugler, Franz 142

Laet, Johannes de 105
Lafitau, Joseph-François 74
Lahille, Fernand 30, 31
Lambroso, Cesare 50
Lassus, J.-B. 46
Laudonnière, René de 121
Laviarde, Achille 21
Le Bon, Gustave 35-6
Le Moyne de Morgues, Jacques 121
Leo X, Pope 9
Leonardi da San Gimignano, Vincenzo
    129
Léry, Jean de 70, 74
Lestringant, F. 119, 121, 122
Letourneau, Charles 30-31
Ligozzi, Jacopo 12
Lipsius, Justus 116
London, Lambeth Palace Library,
    drawings at *44, 46, 48, 49, 51, 54, 55*,
    56
Lubomirski, Prince Albert (pseud.) 121
Lüdingworth, Germany, church at 15
Ludolf, Hiob 101

Madrid, parc del Buen Retiro 31
Magalhães, Fernão de 22
Magellan, Ferdinand 11, 38
Mahu, Jacques 39
Maître, Maurice *5*, 26-7, 36
Malipiero, Ottaviano 132
Manouvrier, Léonce 29
Manuel I, King of Portugal 9
Martial, Captain Louis 30
Martyr, Peter 21
Maximilian I, Holy Roman Emperor 90
Medici, Catherine de' 116
Mendoza, Antonio de 102
Mexico City
    Hospital de la Raza *88*, 130
    National Palacio *86*, 125
    Templo Mayor 125
Miscellanea Cleyeri 42, 43, 56
Möller, Lise Lotte 82
Montaigne, Michel de 74, 119, 120, 128
Montecuhzoma, Aztec ruler 13, 22, *77*,
    79, 106, 107, 112, 117, 118, 122
Montesquieu, Charles de Secondat,
    Baron de 74
Moreau, Gustave 46-7
Mostaert, Jan *70*, 81, 98-9

Nacol-Absou ('the cannibal king') 107,
    74
Needham, Rodney 74
New York, New Museum of
    Contemporary Art 50
Nicol, Paul 30
Nicolay, Nicolas de 120
Nielsen, C. *2*, 34
Noort, Olivier van 22
North, Sir Thomas 122

O'Gorman, Juan 126
Olmos, Andrés de 105
Ortelius, Abraham *17*, 38
Orurdelicone, *see* Button, Jemmy
Ovid (Publius Ovidius Naso) 82
Oviedo y Valdés, Gonzalo Fernández de
    80
Oxford, Bodleian Library 102, 104

Panofsky, Erwin 13
Paracoussi, king of the Platte region *76*,
    107, 118-19
Paraousti Satouriona, king of Florida *81*,
    113-16, 118, 132

Paré, Ambroise 122
Paris
    Chilean Expo pavilion (1882) *3*, *4*, 26
    Galerie Indienne (1845) 45
    Jardin d'Acclimatation *1*, *8-12*, *14*,
      19, 20, 21, 23, 24, 29, 30, 43, 47, 81
    Musée de l'Homme 10, 90
    Société d'Anthropologie 29, 30
    Société d'Ethnographie 29
Parkinson, Sydney 42
Peake, Robert 93
Perkins, Corporal 91
Petit, Pierre *7*, *8-12*, 31, 35
Philip II, King of Spain 129
Picq, Henri 26
Piero di Cosimo 98
Pigafetta, Antonio 39
Piggott, Stuart 93-4, 96
Pignoria, Lorenzo 132-8, 140, 143
Pliny the Elder (Gaius Plinius
    Secundus) 88, 116
Pliny the Younger (Gaius Plinius
    Caecilius Secundus) 142, 146
Plutarch 122, 123, 129
Poe, Edgar Allan 101
Poeschel, S. 85
Polo, Marco 11
Poma de Ayala, Guaman 112
Pope, Lady Elizabeth 93
Pope, Sir William 93
Potgieter, Barent Jansz. *19-21*, 39
Pozzo, Cassiano dal 18, 129, 130
Préault, Auguste 46
Prokosch, Frederic 78
Psalmanaazaar, George *45*, *47*, *50*, *52-3*,
    56, *56*, 68-79, *57*
Puranen, Jorma 17
Purchas, Samuel 72, 104, 121

Quoniambec, Tupinamba chief *75*, 96,
    107, 116, 117, 122

Raphael (Raffaello Santi) 9, 10, 81
Redon, Odilon 24, *29-32*, 47, 55
Reichek, Elaine *36*, 53
Ribeira, park at 9
Ricci, Matteo 72
Rios, Pedro de los 132, 136
Ripa, Cesare 38
Rivera, Diego 16, *86*, *88*, 125-9
Roger, Barthélemy-Joseph-Fuloran *97*
Rome

Accademia dei Lincei 129
Biblioteca Angelica 132, 136
Domus Aurea 97, 98
Vatican 9, 10, 81, 133
Villa Giulia 83
Villa Madama 10
Rotz, Jean 94
Rouillé, Guillaume 116

Sachsen-Weimar, Duke of 101
Saint-Hilaire, Albert 19
Saint-Hilaire, Isidore-Geoffroy 19
Sand, George (Aurore Dupin, Baronne
    Dudevant) 45, 46
Santa Maria island, Strait of Magellan
    22, 42
Santiago
    Museo Artequín *4*, 26
    Museo de Bellas Artes 50
Saussure, Ferdinand de 144
Saussure, Horace-Benedict de 144
Schedel, Hartmann *67*
Schweers, Captain 24
Selden, John 104
Selk'nam (Ona), Fuegian people 22, 26,
    30, 36
Serlio, Sebastiano 95
Settala, Lodovico 18
Shakespeare, William 122
Sigismund II Augustus 84
Sigüenza y Góngora, Carlos de 122
Simcoe, Colonel John Graves 93
Sloan, John 15
Sluperius, Johannes 120
Snow, Captain W. Parker 51
South America Missionary Society 30
Stradanus *see below* Straet, Jan van der
Straet, Jan van der 12, *18*
Sturtevant, William 80, 81, 92-7, 106,
    120
Surinamese people *15*, 36
Sylvester family 95

Tenochtitlán 11, *71*, 102
Thévenot, Melchisedec *73*, 105
Thevet, André 16, *58*, 73, 81, 96, 102-04,
    105, 106, 107, 112, *80*, 116-23, 125,
    128-9, 131-2
Thiry, Léonard *59*, 83, 85-6, 97
Thompson, Cornet 91
Tierra del Fuego 10, 11, 16, 22-3
Tilantongo 101

Tipping, Thomas, monument to 99
Tupac Amaru, Diego Betancur 125
Tupinamba (Brazilian people), and
    cultural artefacts 90-91, 92, 94, 96, 99
Tylor, E. B. 14

Uccello, Paulo 128

Varenius 77
Varro, Marcus Terentius 116
Vasari, Giorgio 116
Vattemare, Hippolyte 46
Vecellio, Cesare 120
Venale, Pietro 83
Villegagnon 102
Virginia Company, The 93

Wahlen, Johann Wilhelm 24
Warburg, Aby 13-15, 16
Warburton, William 105
Watson, Sir Thomas 93
Weert, Sebald de 22, 42
Weiditz, Christoph 89, 91, 120
Winghe, Philip van 135-6
Wittkower, Rudolf 11-12, 88, 102
Wolfeton House, Charminster, Dorset
    100
Woodward, John, 75-6
Workers' Educational Association, The
    91
Worm, Olaus 101

Yahgan, people of Tierra del Fuego 16

Zeroboabel, Formosan prophet 71
Zorzi, Alessandro 89
Zurich, Plattengarten 25